COUNTRYSIDE BOOKS
NEWBURY BERKSHIRE

First published 2010

COUNTRYSIDE BOOKS
3 Catherine Road
Newbury, Berkshire

To view our complete range of books,
please visit us at
www.countrysidebooks.co.uk

ISBN 978 1 84674 214 9

To Evan, Isaac and Flynn

Designed by Peter Davies, Nautilus Design
Produced through MRM Associates Ltd., Reading
Printed by Information Press, Oxford

Contents

Acknowledgements

It is impossible to write a book such as this, without a lot of help. Sometimes that help can be just a chance, brief encounter. An example of this was the young policeman in Rempstone who came across me parked in the village studying an old OS map. The constable not only gave me excellent directions, he also suggested several other locations that I could visit.

At the other end of the scale is my wife Anne, who has spent many, many hours on the project. This has varied from chauffeuring me around the length and breadth of Nottinghamshire – on one occasion to look for a London Underground train (I am sure that she thought that I had 'lost the plot' until we eventually found it!) – to reading my scripts, correcting my grammar, and keeping me focused on the important social history aspects of my brief.

Between the Rempstone bobby and Anne there have been many, many more …

My son John has dragged his 'old man' into the 21st century by helping me get up to speed with AutoCad so that I could produce the maps for the book. I had been 'fluent' in an alternative, but now sadly obsolete CAD (Computer Aided Design) system before I retired. As AutoCad is now the industry standard I decided to take the plunge … and John has certainly kept me afloat and stopped me from drowning in its complexities.

Charlotte McCarthy, the Senior Archivist of the Boots UK Archive, has been a star too. She seems to have left no stone unturned in searching through the records in her care to fill in the details of the Boots staff outings related in Chapter 9.

The staff at Nottinghamshire's Local Studies Libraries, the Durban House Museum at Eastwood and the National Railway Museum's excellent Search Engine have all been most helpful and provided a lot of very useful information.

Photographs play a very important part of a book such as this and I have been fortunate that two long standing and very good friends, Richard Stevens and Frank Berridge, have placed their entire collections of Nottinghamshire steam at my disposal. For me, it was almost like Dracula being parachuted into a blood bank. Both Richard and Frank offered me the use of so many superb images, that it was almost impossible to choose.

I have also used images from the Science and Society Picture Library and the Record Office for Leicestershire, Leicester and Rutland, the staff of both of which have been most helpful. Last, but by no means least, Nick Tomlinson and his team from the excellent Picture the Past image library who have supplied photographs from their vast collection.

Abbreviations

ANB&EJR	Ambergate, Nottingham, Boston & Eastern Junction Railway
BR	British Railways
BTC	British Transport Commission
BW&Co	Barber, Walker & Company (mine owners)
CEGB	Central Electricity Generating Board
CLC	Cheshire Lines Committee (joint GCR, GNR and MR)
CME	Chief Mechanical Engineer
ECML	East Coast Main Line
GCR	Great Central Railway
GCR(N)	Great Central Railway (Nottingham)
GER	Great Eastern Railway
GNR	Great Northern Railway
HL	High Level
L&S	Leicester & Swannington Railway
L&Y	London & York Railway
LD&ECR	Lancashire, Derbyshire & East Coast Railway
LL	Low Level
LMR	London Midland Region (of British Railways)
LMS	London Midland & Scottish Railway
LNER	London & North Eastern Railway
LNWR	London & North Western Railway
M&P	Mansfield & Pinxton Railway
MBM&MJR	Manchester, Buxton, Matlock & Midlands Junction Railway
MCR	Midland Counties Railway
MPD	Motive Power Depot
MR	Midland Railway
MS&LR	Manchester, Sheffield & Lincolnshire Railway
NCB	National Coal Board
NET	Nottingham Express Tramway
NSR	Nottingham Suburban Railway
RCH	Railway Clearing House
RCTS	Railway Correspondence & Travel Society
REC	Railway Executive Committee (who ran the railways during both world wars).
ROD	Railway Operating Department (of the Royal Engineers)
SA&MR	Sheffield, Ashton-under-Lyne & Manchester Railway
SER	South Eastern Railway
SR	Southern Railway
SYJR	South Yorkshire Joint Railway

NOTTINGHAMSHIRE RAILWAYS

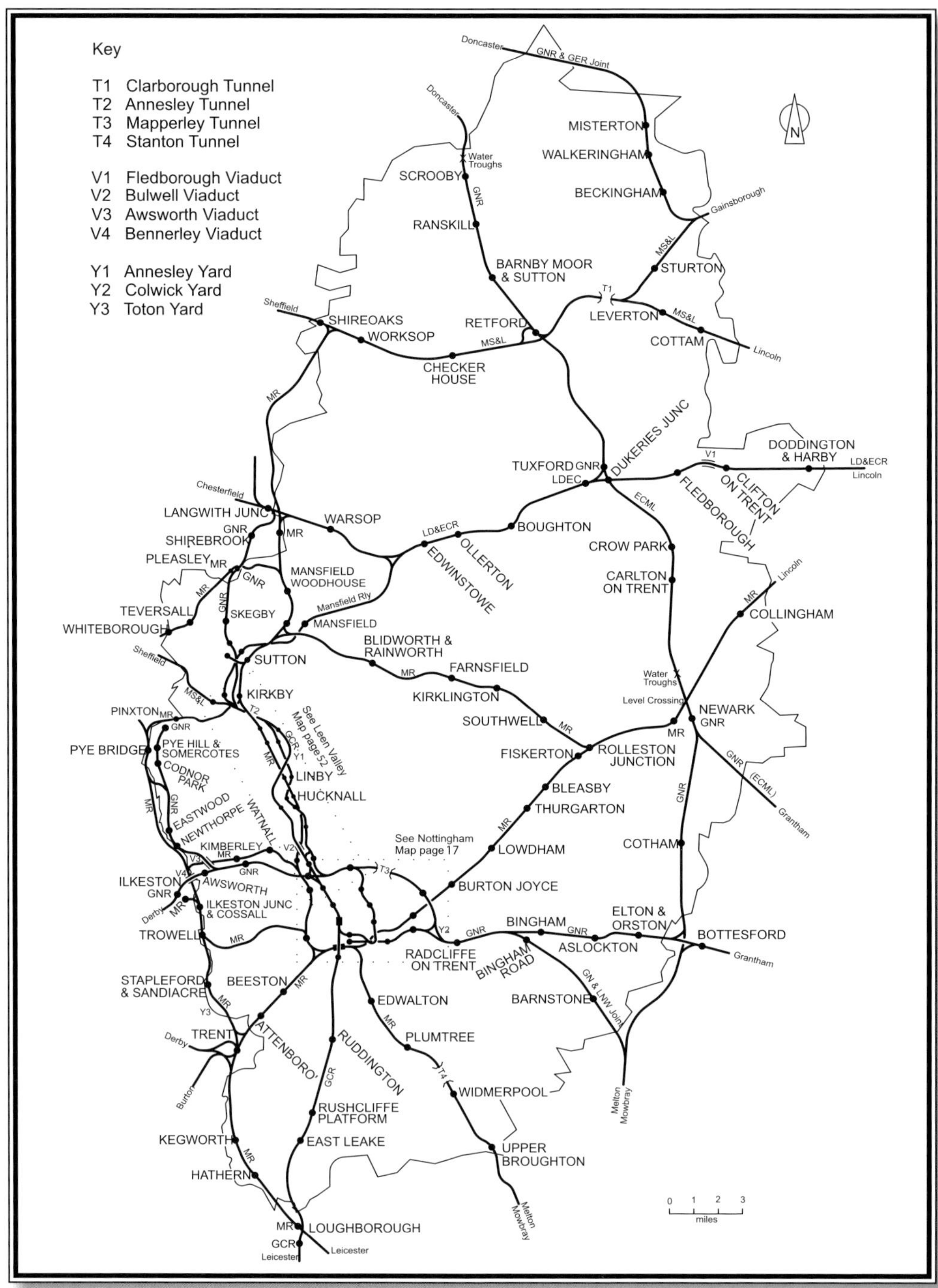

Nottinghamshire's Railways in the golden years just prior to the First World War. (Colliery and freight lines have been omitted for clarity.)

I

Robin Hood County

The mere mention of Nottingham or Nottinghamshire and my guess is that most people will automatically think of Robin Hood. It is not really surprising. What began as a few medieval folk stories about a character of rather dubious authenticity has, over the years, mushroomed into countless movies and TV serials, so that Robin Hood, the Sheriff of Nottingham, Sherwood Forest and Nottinghamshire are now known virtually the whole world over. Just in case anyone has forgotten, the County Council have erected welcome signs on virtually every road entering the county, which proclaim that Nottinghamshire ***IS*** Robin Hood County. The signs on the M1 motorway are huge. But as we shall see in the following pages, there is a lot more to its 834 square miles than just the over-hyped and in reality the probably fictional leader of a medieval gang of hoodlums.

In no particular order of importance, and not necessarily even mentioned in the text: Lace, Lord Byron, Raleigh bicycles, Brian Clough, Coal, D.H. Lawrence, Player's cigarettes, William Booth (founder of the Salvation Army), Bramley apples, Boots the Chemists and Torvill & Dean, to name just a few, have all, to some degree, contributed to the county's very rich history.

Railways too have played an important part. Indeed, Britain's very first 'rayleway', albeit a crude wagonway, was built in 1604 to carry coal from the mines at Strelley to Wollaton (both of which are only a few miles from the centre of Nottingham). It was the brainchild of the flamboyantly named Huntingdon Beaumont. A member of an aristocratic Leicestershire family, Beaumont was a successful and innovative mining engineer. Sadly, he was a hopeless businessman. Over the years he lost enormous sums of money and died a pauper in Nottingham Gaol in 1624 after being incarcerated for debt. Yet his legacy, the concept of guiding wheels by rails, was subsequently adopted by later engineers, including the likes of Isambard Kingdom Brunel and George Stephenson, and became the basis of the world's railways system today.

Nottinghamshire was also the birthplace of the Midland Railway, which eventually grew, prior to the grouping in 1923, to be the third largest railway company in the UK. The Midland's trunk routes in the county – Nottingham to Derby, Nottingham to Lincoln, Nottingham to Mansfield, Long Eaton to Leicester and Long Eaton to Sheffield – are still all vital and busy arteries of today's national railway network.

Nearly 230 years separate Huntingdon Beaumont's wagonway from the birth of the Midland Railway. Between them there is a common denominator, which will recur many times during this narrative. That common denominator is coal. As already noted, the 1604 line carried coal from the mines at Strelley to Wollaton.

The Erewash (which is pronounced erry-wash) Valley, which lies partly in Nottinghamshire and partly in Derbyshire, was a major source of coal. Much of that coal found its way to Leicester via the Erewash Canal, the River Trent and the River Soar Navigation. For many years, the Erewash coalmasters enjoyed a virtual monopoly of coal sales some 30 miles away in Leicester, in spite of there being rich coal measures only a dozen miles or so away, in the area around Swannington and Coalville. The difference lay in the means of transport. Erewash coal was conveyed relatively cheaply by canal. Leicestershire coal arrived in the county town on packhorses or in horse-drawn carts, the cost of which was considerably more than canal-borne coal.

To try to 'level the playing field' the Leicestershire mine owners built their own waterway, the Charnwood Forest Canal. But following the catastrophic failure of one of the feeder reservoirs, the canal closed. Undeterred, the mine owners began to look elsewhere for salvation. This they eventually found in the railway entrepreneur George Stephenson, whose star was already rapidly in the ascendancy.

The outcome was the Leicester & Swannington Railway, one of the country's first 'proper' steam railways, which opened on 17th July 1832. For the Leicestershire coalmasters their support of the L&S proved to be a shrewd move. After the railway opened, their sales soared as the price of coal in Leicester plummeted by 70%.

The citizens of Leicester celebrated.

But in the colliery boardrooms on the Nottinghamshire and Derbyshire borders, the alarm bells were ringing loudly. Pleas by the Erewash coalmasters to the canal proprietors to significantly reduce their tolls on Leicester-bound coal fell on deaf ears.

So the coalmasters sought revenge.

Just a month after the L&S opened, the coalmasters' regular meeting, at the Sun Inn at Eastwood, was dominated by one topic … the building of their own railway. The outcome was the proposal to build the Midland Counties Railway from the Erewash Valley to Leicester, with branches to Derby and Nottingham in order to secure their coal sales there too. Although the plan received considerable local

The Sun Inn at Eastwood, the birthplace of the Midland Railway in 1832, seen here over 100 years later in the 1940s with an impressive line up of contemporary cars parked outside. The Sun dates back to 1750 and prior to the momentous meeting of the Erewash coalmasters here on 16th August 1832, the establishment had already gained a degree of notoriety following an incident in 1797 when part of the inn's floor and some adjoining outbuildings collapsed due to subsidence from earlier coal mining activities. The inn is still in business today, quite recognisable although some windows have been added and it is now marooned on one side of a large traffic island. This gyratory scheme involved the demolition of the building on the right of the photograph – the long-established Machin & Hartwell hardware shop. Note the beautiful wooden wheelbarrow and 'dolly-tub' on display outside. (Courtesy of Nottinghamshire County Council and Picture the Past)

support, there was a shortfall in the required capital. In desperation, the coalmasters turned to the so called 'Liverpool Party,' a group of influential and wealthy Lancashire entrepreneurs, for support.

However, the far-sighted Lancastrians could see the proposed Midland Counties Railway in a somewhat different light ... not as a coal carrying railway, but part of a strategic north–south passenger network. So in return for the Liverpool Party's support, the MCR promoters had to abandon the Erewash Valley part of the proposed line in preference to the Nottingham to Derby line from which (near Long Eaton) would spring a line, not only to Leicester, but then onwards to Rugby to an interchange with the London to Birmingham line.

To put this a little more into perspective, although it is outside the geographical boundaries of this narrative, George Stephenson, who was the darling of the Lancastrian entrepreneurs, and his son Robert were deeply involved with the construction of the North Midland Railway from Derby to Leeds. This, in the Liverpool Party's eyes, was the next link in which was then a rather roundabout north–south chain: Leeds, Derby, Rugby, London.

The fact that their long time rival Derby was on the main line and that Nottingham was only served by a branch line was not well received by the city fathers. But from 4th June 1839 when the MCR line from Derby opened, Nottingham was on the railway map. It was something that some other comparable sized towns and cities still had to wait for many years to achieve.

Before looking further at the development of railways in the county, mention must be made of another pioneer, the Mansfield & Pinxton Railway. This was an 8 mile long, 4' 4" gauge horse drawn tramway, which opened, to the accompaniment of much local celebration, in April 1819. Although it was intended to carry coal to the canal for onward shipment, most of the traffic on the M&P was **to** Mansfield, which was in the opposite direction.

The M&P was eventually absorbed by the Midland Railway in 1848. But prior to losing its independence, the line's main claim to fame was that it carried thousands of tons of locally quarried magnesian limestone blocks on the first part of their journey to London where they were used in the building of the Houses of Parliament.

As it stood, it must be said that the M&P was not of much practical use to the Midland. Not only was it the wrong gauge, the formation was in places too weak. More importantly, the original route had avoided obstacles by circumnavigation rather than by confrontation. This resulted in it having numerous twists and turns that were far too tight for a standard gauge passenger line. Yet, thanks to the Midland's improvements, much of the M&P route is still in use today.

One can only speculate to quantify the millions, if not billions, of tons of coal that have passed over the route since the first horse drawn wagon loads (which were ceremonially burnt in Mansfield's Market Place) arrived in the town nearly 200 years ago.

2

OLD KING COAL

Nottinghamshire lies on the top of a vast coalfield, the fuel from which has been utilised since at least Roman times. The advent of canals in the latter part of the 18th century enabled wider markets to be exploited. However, the final 'pieces in the jigsaw' were provided by the railways. The story of the county's railways and the development of the mining industry are inextricably linked.

On the western flank of the county, the Erewash Valley and beyond into Derbyshire, the coal lies fairly close to the surface. This is what geologists term an 'exposed coalfield'. In places known as 'outcrops' the coal was actually to be found at ground level. But as these outcrops became worked out, resort had to be made to digging 'bell pits', which were holes in the ground down to the level of the coal seam. These were then hollowed out in the shape of a bell.

Travelling eastwards through the county, the coal measures become progressively deeper and deeper, which in geological terms makes it now a 'concealed coalfield'. To get some idea of the degree of this 'concealment', the shafts at Bevercotes Colliery, the last and the most easterly Nottinghamshire colliery, which was sunk by the National Coal Board in 1963, needed to be over 3,000 feet (1,000 metres) in depth, to reach the coal seams. Perhaps an alternative and maybe a more understandable description is to say that the Bevercotes shafts were over ½ mile deep.

Coal is a generic term, as for instance is 'beer' and 'washing powder'. So, like beers and washing powders, there are many different varieties. Coal comes from different seams. In the Nottinghamshire coalfield these seams included Top Hard, Deep Hard, Deep Soft, Tupton, Thick Black Shale, First Piper, Kilburn and Silkstone, to name but a few. Each seam had its own characteristic properties. Coal for domestic use was different to the coal supplied to the railways as loco coal. Similarly the country's numerous Gas Light & Coke Companies demanded coal with different properties to loco or domestic coal.

More importantly, during the age of steam in Nottinghamshire, the coal mines were major employers. In 1896, Her Majesty's Mines Inspector's annual report noted that there were 46 mines in operation. These directly employed a total of 18,000 men working underground with a further 4,700 working on the surface. To these must be

Between 1923 and 1948, the publicity conscious London Midland & Scottish Railway commissioned many contemporary artists to produce artwork for their posters. Not only did these feature the numerous resorts, beauty spots and tourist attractions served by the LMS, the company also promoted its ancillary activities including maritime services, infrastructure maintenance and, as illustrated above, its most important mineral traffic, coal. This particular commission from around 1935 was entrusted to one of the most outstanding and, I have to confess, one of my favourite artists of the period, Sir Norman Wilkinson R.I. (1878–1971). Whilst the poster is rather anonymously titled 'A Midland Coalfield' it is obviously based on either an actual colliery, or a freelance composition derived from an amalgam of images in his sketchbook. But whatever its origins, it is a powerful picture with the skyline dominated by the towering headstocks that were once a familiar sight in many Nottinghamshire mining towns and villages. Add to that the miners heading for home after a long, hard shift, carrying their empty 'snap tins' – East Midlands speak for lunch boxes – and the picture is complete.
(National Railway Museum/Science and Society Picture Library)

added the hundreds, if not thousands, employed to transport the coal, particularly by rail, to its final destination.

The importance of coal in the age of steam cannot be overstated. It was the lifeblood of the country's economy. For a start, none of the country's 20,000-plus main line steam locomotives could have moved without it. Ditto the thousands of static steam engines that provided power for the nation's mills and factories. On the domestic front, coal was used for both heating and cooking. Some early prototype gas fired cooking ranges had been exhibited at the Great Exhibition of 1851. But gas cooking did not make any significant inroads into the domestic market until after the turn of the last century, due to both the fear of explosions and health scares about eating food cooked in an atmosphere potentially contaminated with lethal carbon monoxide fumes. But even when gas did become an accepted fuel for cooking, it has to be remembered that in those days it was a derivative of coal. Coal gas lamps illuminated streets, homes and factories.

Coke, a by-product of the coal distillation process that produced the gas, was an essential ingredient in the manufacture of iron and steel. Another vital by-product was coal tar, which had several uses. Perhaps the most important is when it is combined with a suitable stone aggregate to provide 'tarmac' … still the basis for the nation's roads today.

It is impossible to accurately quantify the number of coal mines that have existed in Nottinghamshire. As old ones were worked out and uneconomic mines closed, new and more efficient ones opened. As noted earlier, in 1896, there were 46 mines in operation. But whilst doing the research for this chapter I have identified at least 70 collieries that were in operation at various times during the golden years of railways in the county. Even that is probably the tip of the iceberg. An example of the complexity of the subject can perhaps be illustrated by the fact that there are records showing that within a one mile radius of the former Brinsley Colliery near Eastwood, there are over 100 other known mine shafts, some dating back over 200 years.

Brinsley Colliery (1872–1970) was where the novelist D.H. Lawrence's father worked. By 1930 the coal reserves had been exhausted but the shafts remained open for another 40 years to provide access to neighbouring mines. This practice of combining with other, originally separate, mines was not uncommon and provides another imponderable variable in the 'numbers game'.

Brinsley was one of several collieries in the Eastwood area owned by Barber, Walker & Company, which was one of the county's biggest mine owners. Whilst not perfect, it seems to have been one of the better employers. Indeed, D.H. Lawrence was born and spent his early life in houses that had been built by the company in Eastwood in the 1850s to accommodate its employees.

This policy of providing homes for employees culminated in the 1920s when

BW&Co purchased over 300 acres of land at Bircotes, in the north of the county, on which it built over 1,000 houses for miners at the new Harworth Colliery. Other Nottinghamshire communities such as New Ollerton, Forest Town, Warsop Vale, and Langold were all originally spawned by various other mine owners to house their employees.

This photograph of Brinsley Colliery was taken in 1913 by the Rector of Eastwood, the Rev F.W. Cobb. His legacy is a collection of unique images of colliery life, including many below ground, some even at the coalface itself. Towering over this scene are the tandem timber headstocks, which dated back to the opening of the mine in 1872. After it closed in 1970, they were dismantled for preservation. Following closure, the site was landscaped and transformed into an attractive picnic area. The finishing touches were added in 1991 when, following a joint initiative by British Coal and Nottinghamshire County Council, the restored headstocks were returned to their original position.
(Courtesy of Nottinghamshire County Council and Picture the Past)

Barber, Walker & Co can trace its history back to 1680 and by the dawn of the 20th century, it had a virtual monopoly of pits in the immediate vicinity of Eastwood. In addition to Brinsley, BW&Co's other collieries included Moor Green, High Park, Watnall and Underwood.

'The loop of fine chain' referred to Barber Walker's extensive private railway system, which connected its various collieries to each other and also to the company's land sale wharfs in Eastwood and Watnall Cantelupe. The western end of the line, which was over 8 miles in length, connected with both the Midland and Great Northern Railways' Erewash Valley lines near Langley Mill. At the eastern end, near Watnall, there were additional connections to both the MR and GNR. This resulted in wagons bearing the inscription 'B W & Co' being a familiar sight in many parts of the country. During one period BW&Co operated 'passenger' trains, which carried their employees to and from private stations near their homes to whichever mine they worked in.

A section of the M1 motorway, between junctions 26 and 27, now runs along the course of part of the eastern leg of BW&Co's private line. For many years, the site was easily recognisable by the four 200 ft high chimneys close to the eastern side of the motorway. These chimneys, which were a familiar landmark until they were demolished in August 2009, were the remnants of the former BW&Co's Watnall Brickworks, which was adjacent to the company's Watnall Colliery.

The brickworks was rather unusual in that the bricks it produced were not made from clay. The basic ingredient was actually colliery spoil, which was crushed into a very fine powder. This powder was then mixed with water, poured into moulds under pressure and fired in the kilns for two weeks. The resulting bricks – known in the trade as 'commons' – were not top quality, but they were suitable for building internal walls and so on in a similar way that 'breeze blocks' are used today.

The majority of the spoil came from the Moor Green Colliery. Every afternoon, ten or so wagons loaded with spoil would arrive at the brickworks behind one of BW&Co's fleet of steam locomotives. After stabling the incoming wagons, the little engine would collect the empty wagons from the previous day's spoil train and then bustle back along the 2½ miles to Moor Green.

A surprisingly large proportion of the route was through some pleasant pastoral countryside and passed within sight of the ruins of the historic Beauvale Priory. Founded in 1343, the monks held the rights to the coal mining activities in the area. Following the dissolution of the priory in 1540, the structure fell into disrepair, but the part that still survives was subsequently incorporated into a farm.

But I cannot help but wonder whether, during the days of steam, the spirits of the priory's long departed monks perhaps took time out from their ghostly devotions to watch, with interest, the comings and goings on Barber Walker's little railway.

3

This is Nottingham

In the earliest records relating to Nottingham it was referred to as 'Tigguocobauc', which translated from ancient British means the 'house of caves'. These caves were subsequently colonised by an Anglo-Saxon tribe whose leader had what is today the very un-PC name of 'Snot'. After one or two subtle changes in the spelling the settlement became known as 'Snottingham', which literally means the 'home of the Snots'. But before moving on from this piece of historical trivia, I must point out that in Anglo-Saxon times 'snot' meant 'wise'.

We must fast forward to more recent history …

As noted in Chapter 1, Nottingham's city fathers were pleased that the arrival of the Midland Counties Railway in 1839 had put their town on the railway map. But their enthusiasm was tempered by the fact that it was only at the end of a branch line. Even more galling was the fact that their near neighbour and traditional rival, Derby, was on the main railway network.

In this respect, the MCR did itself no favours by only building a terminal (rather than a through) station, which was located on the west side of Carrington Street. This rather underlined Nottingham's branch line status, and in retrospect, it proved to be a short sighted decision.

In 1846, by which time the MCR had been amalgamated into the Midland Railway, the latter opened the Nottingham and Lincoln line, still using the original MCR station. This resulted in a somewhat 'messy' operating arrangement in that trains from and to Lincoln had to reverse in and out of the platforms. This lasted for almost two years until the Midland, who had recognised the MCR's mistake, opened a second, this time a through station, on Station Street in May 1848. Later that year, the MR line north along the Leen Valley opened as far as Kirkby, and 12 months later the same line reached Mansfield.

But the council were still 'miffed' by happenings just 16 miles away. The Midland had rather rubbed salt into Nottingham's wounds by deciding to make their headquarters

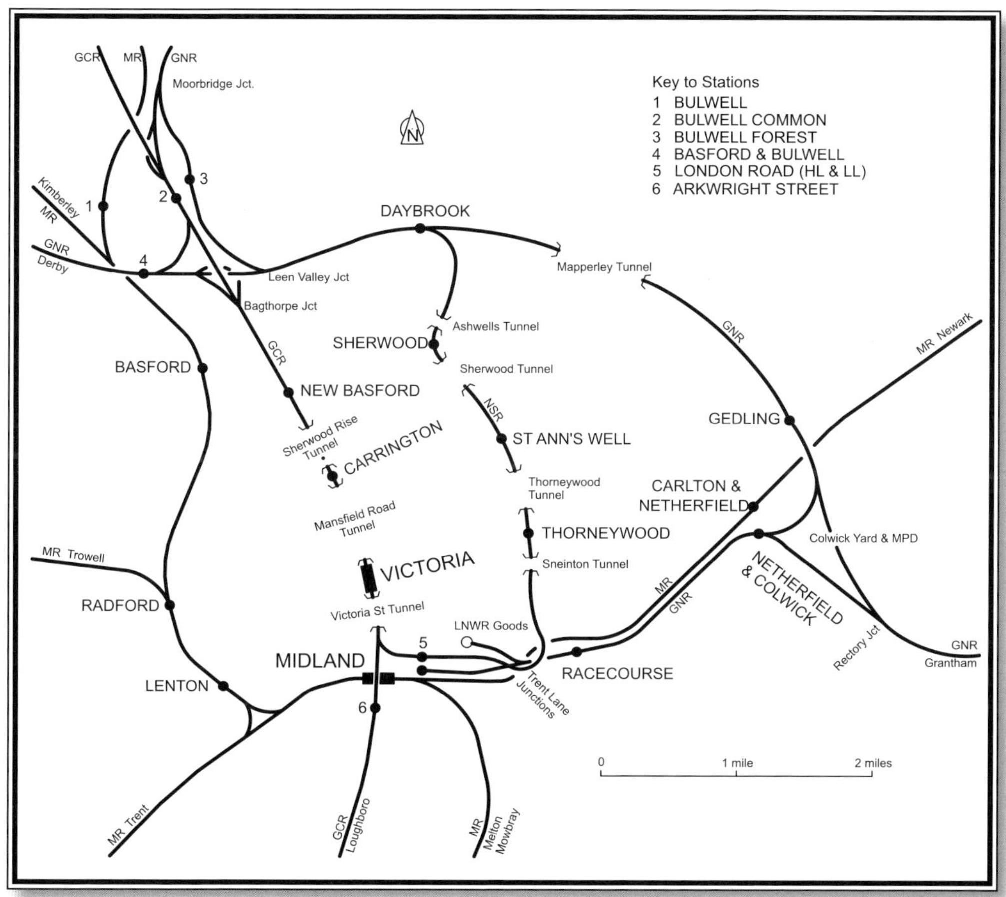

A map of Nottingham's railways when at their zenith in the early years of the 20th century.

in Derby. Nottingham's answer was to form a Council Railway Committee charged with actively encouraging the promotion of new trunk railways through the town. (Nottingham was then still a town. It did not become a city until Queen Victoria bestowed the appropriate Letters Patent during her Jubilee Year in 1897.)

One such scheme that attracted the committee's attention was the Ambergate, Nottingham, Boston & Eastern Junction Railway. From Boston, it was proposed that the line would run almost due west through Grantham to Nottingham and then turn north-west to Ambergate (in Derbyshire) where it would link up with the equally verbosely named Manchester, Buxton, Matlock & Midlands Junction Railway. In theory, if these two schemes came to fruition, Nottingham would lie on a main east to west rail artery.

Although the story of the MBM&MJR is outside the geographical scope of this volume, suffice to say here that it only built the first nine miles from Ambergate to Rowsley at which point the money ran out. But at Ambergate, its junction was aligned so that it would allow through running from the ANB&EJR if, and when, it arrived.

But it never did because it too was experiencing serious financial difficulties, such that only the central section between Grantham and Nottingham came to be built. Even then the last two or three miles into Nottingham were over Midland Railway metals through running powers from Colwick, which enabled the newcomer access to the 1848 station. The Midland's ambivalence to the arrangement was because it saw the ANB&EJR as potentially becoming a part of its own empire.

An atmospheric view looking west along Station Street a few years before the close of the 19th century, taken from the then brand new GCR bridge. Part of the Midland's 1848 station can be seen on the left of the photograph, beyond which is part of the bridge carrying Carrington Street over the MR tracks. In the centre background are the Midland Railway's Goods Offices, which have now been reincarnated as the Coroner's Court. To the left of this are two of the four gables of the now demolished two-storey Midland Goods and Grain Depot. It was a massive building, the total floor space being well over an acre. Every vehicle in the photograph is horse drawn.
(Courtesy of R.H. Bird and Picture the Past)

It came as quite a shock therefore when the Midland's proposal of marriage was turned down, primarily because one of the major shareholders in the ANB&EJR also happened to be a director of the Great Northern Railway. This was one of the East Coast Main Line companies (see Chapter 8) and had opened from a temporary station in London as far as Peterborough in 1850. Two years later it extended its so called 'Towns Line' north, which included a connection with the ANB&EJR at Grantham. By this time the GNR terminus at Kings Cross had also opened and the company was beginning to plan an assault on the Midland's monopoly in the Nottinghamshire & Derbyshire coalfield.

The 20 or so miles of the ANB&EJR, which was worked by the GNR, provided that company with the stepping stone towards the heart of the East Midlands. But the stage was already set for trouble.

The Battle of Nottingham

In the early 1850s, to get from Nottingham to London via the Midland Railway, passengers first had to travel to Derby. From here they travelled via Leicester to Rugby where, yet again, a change of trains was involved before eventually arriving at Euston.

So the 'cat was really set amongst the pigeons' when the ANB&EJR announced a much quicker ***direct service*** from the Midland's Nottingham station to London (Kings Cross) via Grantham and the GNR. Not surprisingly, the Midland went ballistic. But even legal proceedings in the Court of Chancery and an injunction in favour of the Midland did not deter the service from starting.

From here on, the story could well have been in the plot of a Buster Keaton or a Keystone Cops movie rather than an actual event. The date was 2nd August 1852, the first day of the new quicker, direct joint ANB&EJR and GNR London to Nottingham service ...

This train duly arrived with the through coaches from London. But as the GNR loco began to run round its train ready for the return journey to Grantham, it suddenly found its path blocked by a Midland locomotive. And to make sure that the GNR driver would 'get the message' a second Midland locomotive was following on the run round. In effect, the GNR loco found itself as the 'meat' between two Midland 'slices of bread'. What followed, according to a contemporary report, was similar to an 'elephant hunt'. The GNR driver, realising his predicament, decided that although the odds were heavily stacked against him, at least he would 'go down fighting' and charged the Midland locos.

But it was to no avail. The GNR crew were summarily ejected from their footplate, and the loco was triumphantly towed away by the Midland, who 'imprisoned' it for the next seven months. And to make sure that there would be no clandestine attempts

This view looking east towards the Midland Railway's 1848 station can be fairly accurately dated as being taken in late 1897 or early 1898. The scene is dominated by the massive new 170 ft span bowstring girder bridge that was to carry the Great Central's London Extension over the Midland's premises. The first trains rumbled over the bridge in July 1898, but contractor's plant was still occupying the bridge when the photograph was taken.
(Courtesy of Nottingham Historical Film Unit and Picture the Past)

to liberate the loco, the MR removed the rails in front of the shed where it had been incarcerated. In the meantime, the MR and GNR lawyers had a field day as they embarked on their own brand of elephant hunt in the courts.

As noted earlier, the ANB&EJR had initially gained access to Nottingham thanks to running powers over the Midland from Colwick. But that relationship, to say the least, became rather strained following the arrest and imprisonment of the GNR's locomotive. The ultimate result of the altercation was a 2¾ mile long extension of the ANB&EJR from Colwick to a separate station on London Road. The handsome building, which opened in October 1857, was designed by Thomas Hine, a leading architect in 19th century Nottingham.

The canal bridge, which is hidden by the surging crowds in the photograph, is a so-called 'turnover' or 'roving' bridge. It is at this point that the canal towpath changed from one side of the cut to the other. On one side of the canal there is a straight ramp from the towpath up to the bridge. On the opposite side, the ramp turns through 180°; the net result of the two ramps allows a horse drawing a barge to cross the canal without needing to be detached from the towrope.

In 1855, the ANB&EJR was leased to the GNR, hence the prominent Great

Northern Railway sign fixed high up on the roof as seen in the photograph. In 1860, the company changed its name to the rather more manageable Nottingham & Grantham Railway & Canal Company. The new name reflected the fact that the company owned both the Nottingham Canal and the Grantham Canal as well of course as the railway line between the two towns. Although a GNR adjunct, it remained nominally independent until 1st January 1923 when it became part of the LNER group.

A wonderfully evocative photograph of crowds crossing the canal bridge outside the Great Northern's London Road (later Low Level) station during the Goose Fair in October 1898. The lack of sensitivity of the contemporary photographic emulsions, which were unable to freeze movement, adds an almost mysterious dynamism to the image. It seems that as many people are trying to enter the station as there are heading towards the fair, which until 1928 was held in the Market Square. Dating back over 700 years, it has come a long way from the days when geese were driven from Lincolnshire, Cambridgeshire, and even as far away as Norfolk to be sold – hence the name. The coming of the railways changed all that, and, for a while, local cheeses became one of the main commodities on sale. Today, it is basically just a huge fun fair held over four days at the beginning of October on the Forest Recreation Ground and there isn't a goose to be seen for miles around. That said, cheese is still on sale … but only as an accompaniment to some of the thousands of burgers that are eaten. (S.W.A. Newton photograph reproduced by permission of the Record Office for Leicestershire, Leicester and Rutland)

The GNR expands

I used the words 'stepping stone' rather than 'springboard' for the GNR's incursions into the Midland Railway's heartland deliberately. With the opening of the London Road station, and with the ANB&EJR now firmly in its pocket, the GNR could begin its offensive. But their initial assault, to say the least, was rather curious ...

Derbyshire lies to the ***west*** of Nottinghamshire. The coalfield that the GNR hoped to tap into lay to the ***north*** of Nottingham. So, maybe to confuse the enemy, the GNR incursion began by heading ***east*** out of Nottingham along the ANB&EJR line as far Colwick. From here the new line began to turn through a long and difficult 180° arc through Gedling and the troublesome 1,132 yard long Mapperley Tunnel before reaching Daybrook, where at last, the line was heading in the right direction. That said, to reach Daybrook station, which is a tad over 3 miles north along the A60, Mansfield Road, from the centre of Nottingham, GNR trains had to travel some 7½ miles from London Road station. Midland Railway trains between Nottingham and Derby were approaching the halfway point of their journey after 7½ miles. An equivalent GNR train arriving at Daybrook still had 14 miles to travel before it reached Derby.

The station that never was

As already related, there was a very strong pro-railway lobby within Nottingham's councillors and aldermen. Their primary aim was to boost civic pride by improving both passenger and freight services and facilities. One of the council's main gripes was that the Midland station was over ½ mile from the Market Square. The GNR's terminus on London Road was even further. The latter company had not done themselves any favours in the council's eyes by siting their passenger station in rival Derby on Friargate, which was reasonably convenient to the town centre.

So, in what seems today to be an extraordinary move, in the early 1880s the council decided to take the law into their own hands by proposing a Nottingham Central station, which would have been used jointly by the Midland, the GNR and the LNWR. Had this new station been built, the centre of Nottingham as we know it today would have been entirely different.

The plans were prepared by Edward Parry, the County Surveyor, and his assistant J. Greenhalgh Walker. The names of Parry and Walker are destined to appear several times more in this narrative.

The proposed new station would have been on a west to east alignment from just outside the Theatre Royal and Market Street to Cranbrook Street. Both Upper Parliament Street and Lower Parliament Street would have been moved to the north side of the new site and renamed New Parliament Street. The main access to the station would have been directly from Smithy Row on the north side of the Old Market

Square. To maintain north to south access to the town centre two bridges across the station would have been provided. One would have connected Milton Street with Clumber Street; the other Glasshouse Street and Broad Street. Construction would have caused considerable upheaval as it necessitated the demolition of numerous properties (albeit many classed as 'slums') and the excavation of thousands of tons of earth and rock.

But building the new station was only part of it. Getting trains into and out of it would have involved some even more serious engineering. Several miles of new line, a considerable proportion of which would have been underground through at least four tunnels, would have been necessary. Add to this a 600 yard viaduct on the east side of the station and it will come as no surprise that none of the three railways involved were remotely interested. Of the trio the LNWR was only a minor player. Its sparse passenger service from London Road to Northampton was by virtue of running powers over the GNR from Nottingham to Saxondale Junction and thence out of the county on the GNR & LNWR joint line.

Not surprisingly, the Midland and the GNR were equally unenthusiastic. In those days, when there was little alternative to train travel, neither company could see much point in spending vast sums of money just to satisfy the council's ego by getting involved with the building of a central station. Logic said that if folk wanted to travel they would do so, irrespective of where the nearest station was located. The major investment that would have been involved would not have seen much, if any, increase in passenger revenue. And compared with many villages, where the local railway station was often two, three and sometimes more miles away, Nottingham's residents were comparatively well served.

But as we will see a little later, 15 years on, history was to repeat itself. This time the outcome (Nottingham Victoria) was somewhat more successful. But in between came the Nottingham Suburban Railway.

The Nottingham Suburban Railway

Passenger trains on the new GNR line (which became known locally both as the 'Back Line' and the 'Outer Circle') were regularly subjected to quite serious delays as a result of the volume of freight traffic heading into and out of the company's new marshalling yard at Colwick. Many of these freight trains served the collieries in the Erewash and Leen valleys. But irrespective of which direction they were travelling – loaded coal trains to Colwick or empty wagons being returned to the pits – a stiff climb was involved to the summit at Arno Vale. A number of Nottingham businessmen, recognising the problems on the GNR, proposed a new, shorter line between the GNR's stations at London Road and Daybrook. This new line, which they named the Nottingham Suburban Railway, almost halved the distance between

London Road and Daybrook. It was enthusiastically supported by the town council.

Having canvassed and obtained the support of the GNR, the Nottingham Suburban opened on 2nd December 1889. Although it remained independent until the grouping in 1923, it was worked from the outset by the GNR. With quite commodious stations at Thorneywood, St Ann's Well and Sherwood, the promoters had high hopes of success. Sadly, it was to elude them.

Although the NSR route was three miles shorter than the 'Back Line' it was at the expense of some serious engineering involving even steeper gradients and four tunnels. Northbound trains were faced with a formidable two mile uphill slog, mainly at 1 in 50, to the summit of the line. By the time a train breasted the summit it had climbed over 200 feet. Southbound trains had the slightly easier option of around a mile at 1 in 70 to the summit. But either way required the footplate crews to demonstrate enginemanship of the highest order.

The use of the word 'suburban' was somewhat misleading. Today, due to Nottingham's urban sprawl, describing the route as 'suburban' would be accurate. But when it was built, much of the NSR route was rural. Perhaps it was a speculative venture, in the hope that the railway would encourage house building near the line's stations.

Perhaps, more significantly, one should note that the line's engineer was the County Surveyor, Edward Parry, who was assisted once again by J. Greenhalgh Walker. Parry also happened to be a director of Nottingham Patent Brickworks at Thorneywood whose factory would be connected to the NSR. With the benefit of hindsight I am perhaps being a little disingenuous by suggesting that Parry had a hidden agenda with regard to the NSR. Maybe he saw it as an easy means of reducing his transport costs and reaching a larger market. Or maybe he hoped that the proliferation of new housing estates near the line would provide a ready market for his bricks.

But it has to be said that the 'writing was on the wall' for the little line almost before it had opened. The Manchester, Sheffield & Lincolnshire Railway had already begun its march south towards London (see Chapter 6). And when the MS&LR's London Extension eventually opened through Nottingham ten years later, it destroyed the main *raison d'être* of the NSR. To this must be added the proliferation of the Corporation's electric tramways. One of the tram routes passed over the NSR at Thorneywood station. Another route rumbled under the line outside Daybrook station. The trams, which offered a much more frequent, if not as comfortable means of getting to and from the city centre, proved to be the final nails in the NSR's coffin. The line's passenger stations closed as early as 1916. The remaining few passenger trains that used the NSR as a short cut were withdrawn in 1931.

If there was any faint glimmer of hope of a revival, it was extinguished by Hitler's Luftwaffe during an air raid on Nottingham in May 1941. A bomb blew away part of an NSR embankment and damaged the adjacent bridge over the Midland near Trent Lane Junction. This damage was never properly repaired and for the next 10 years, until the NSR was finally closed in 1951, it was worked as a 'long sidings' from the Daybrook end.

Nottingham Victoria

A more detailed account of the invasion of the Manchester, Sheffield & Lincolnshire Railway (later, the Great Central Railway) into Nottinghamshire is told in Chapter 6. However, this chapter on Nottingham cannot ignore the profound influence that the arrival of the MS&LR had on the city itself.

The arrival of the MS&LR was welcomed with open arms by the council. Their long dreamed of grand central station would at last become a reality. The contract for the construction of the section of the MS&LR's London Extension from Annesley to East Leake had been awarded to Logan & Hemingway, who appointed

This is a view looking south-west from Huntingdon Street and Woodborough Road across the Victoria station construction site in 1899. In the foreground the retaining wall and copings for Platform 10 have been built. Running across the centre of the picture are the wall and copings for Platform 6. Temporary tracks have been laid to facilitate the easier delivery of building materials by rail both to here and other construction sites along the route.
(Courtesy of Nottingham City Council and Picture the Past)

none other than the former County Surveyor, Edward Parry, as the engineer for the section.

The northern approach to the station was via two tunnels, Sherwood Rise and Mansfield Road. As tunnels go, these were relatively easy to construct. At the south of the station the 392 yard long Victoria Street Tunnel was a whole different ball game. Much of it was under existing streets, flanked by commercial properties. The 'cut and cover' section along the line of Thurland Street proved to be particularly difficult and took over a year to complete. The proximity of the cellars of the licensed premises flanking the excavations seems to have had some kind of strange magnetic attraction for the navvies. As a result, the contractor had to pay several thousand pounds in compensation to the landlords of the affected premises, not only for the structural damage to their cellars, but the resulting loss of stock.

As related later in Chapter 6, the MS&LR had completely outwitted the Great Northern with its false promises about not extending beyond Annesley. But having gone for broke with its London Extension, the MS&LR then sought partners to contribute towards sharing in at least small parts of the horrendous costs of construction. The Midland totally rejected the MS&LR's approaches to become involved with their new 'joint' stations at both Nottingham and Leicester. But having recovered from their initial pique at being conned by the MS&LR, the GNR could see some major advantages in 'sharing a bed' with it at the new Nottingham Central station.

The MS&LR London Extension crossed over the GNR's 'Back Line' near Basford, so a link here would allow GNR trains from Derby and Pinxton straight into the heart of Nottingham. Every GNR train that used this link to short circuit the 'Back Line' would both significantly reduce journey times and save some six unnecessary miles. But to maximise on this saving, a second link to the south of the new station to join the existing ANB&EJR line near London Road would be necessary. Constructing the links would be a costly exercise, as was sharing the costs of the new Nottingham joint station. That said, the GNR considered it a worthwhile investment. The short cut would significantly reduce operating costs and the quicker, more convenient, service would hopefully attract more patronage.

The northern link near Basford was at Bagthorpe Junction. GNR trains heading out of Nottingham towards Derby or Pinxton had a simple, slightly rising connection to reach their home metals just prior to Basford & Bulwell station. It was a different story for GNR trains from Derby or Pinxton heading into Nottingham. Soon after leaving Basford & Bulwell, the single line link onto the new line descended quickly at 1 in 100 and then began to turn through 90°. First the link passed under a bridge carrying the old line towards Daybrook. Immediately beyond this was a foul, curving 90 yard long tunnel on a rising 1 in 100 gradient, which burrowed under the MS&LR before joining the new line at Bagthorpe Junction. This tunnel, which was officially

A hive of activity at the south end of Nottingham Victoria in the 1950s.
(Courtesy of F.W. Stevenson and Picture the Past)

Basford Tunnel, was known to the railwaymen who passed through it, and to the poor souls who had to maintain it, as the 'Rat Hole'.

The southern link was simpler, but still involved some serious engineering. Just south of Victoria Street Tunnel the GNR established a junction at Weekday Cross. From here the new GNR line turned east as it headed towards the original ANB&EJR line. Much of this line was on a viaduct.

Naturally, when the brand new joint central station opened on 24th May 1900, the GNR diverted all its passenger traffic from the handsome London Road premises.

It probably goes without saying that the MS&LR, which had changed its name to the Great Central Railway on 1st August 1897, wanted to call the new joint station Nottingham Central. Not surprisingly, the GNR would have none of it, preferring Nottingham Joint Station. Eventually, both parties agreed on the compromise suggested by the Town Clerk. The date of opening, 24th May, also happened to be Queen Victoria's birthday. Naming the new station 'Victoria' was the ideal solution to the problem, subject of course to Her Majesty giving the requisite consent. History shows that that consent was given.

A more detailed account of Victoria station is given in Chapter 6.

London Road (High Level) station

Whilst Nottingham Victoria was ideally situated for the shopping and commercial part of the city, the main sporting venues, the cricket ground at Trent Bridge and the football grounds of Notts County and Nottingham Forest, were, and still are, all located within a stone's throw of each other on the south side of the city. Trent Bridge had hosted its first Test Match (*v* Australia) in 1899. Notts County, formed in 1862, is the world's oldest professional football club. To cater for sports fans, the GNR provided a station on the new viaduct from Weekday Cross, which to avoid confusion with the original GNR station nearby, was named London Road (High Level). To emphasise its purpose the station nameboard proclaimed: 'Alight here for Trent Bridge Cricket and Football Grounds'.

Alighting wasn't a problem.

Waiting for a train was a different ballgame. Sandwiched between the tall Boots Island Street factory on one side and Nottingham Gas Works on the other, London Road High Level must come very close to the top of the list of the country's most miserable railway stations. It was extraordinarily draughty, rather smelly and completely godforsaken. Having waited for trains there, I am speaking from personal experience!

Nottingham Midland station – Mark 3

The opening of the new Victoria station in the city centre provided a timely wake-up call for the Midland to improve the dowdy and long past their best-before date

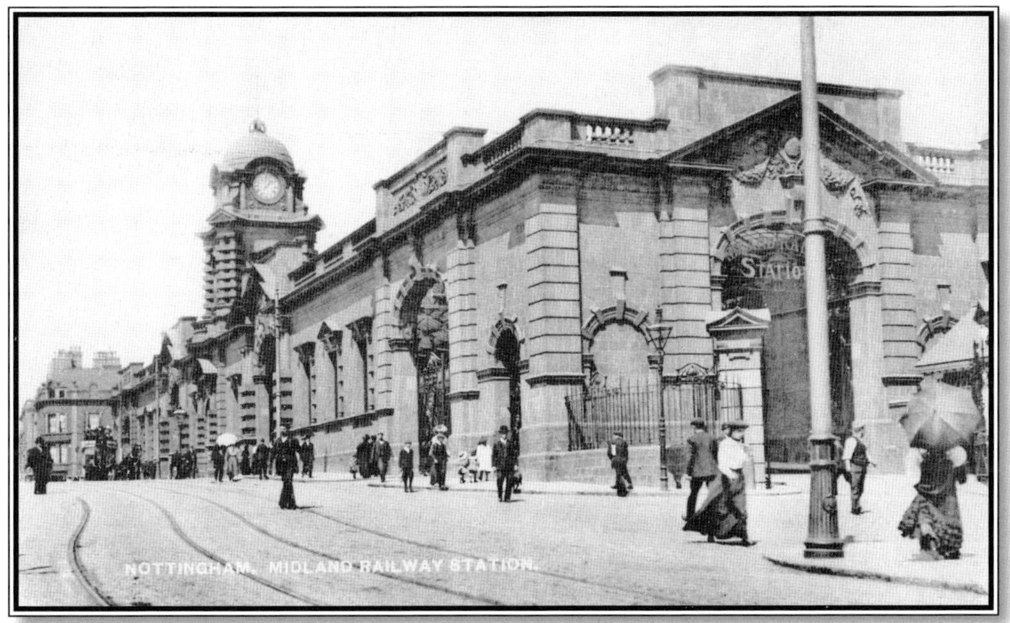

Nottingham's third Midland Railway station, looking north along Carrington Street, circa 1910. The tramlines, the gas lamp and the pole supporting the trolley wires have all disappeared, but beyond that surprisingly little has changed. (Courtesy of Nottingham City Council and Picture the Past)

facilities on Station Street. In fairness, it has to be said that the Midland board's very positive response seems to have been that 'anything the GCR can do, we can do better'. Their starting point was to employ E.A. Lambert, the same architect who had been responsible for the design of Victoria. The access to the new station was to be from Carrington Street, the bridge over which had to be widened and strengthened to accommodate the new buildings.

Architects, like leopards, don't change their spots, so a dedicated student of architecture would have been able to identify some almost identical detail similarities between Victoria and the new Midland stations. But overall, they were as different as chalk and cheese. The 'new' Midland opened without any formal ceremony on 17th January 1904. Lambert's Neo-Baroque-style buildings and the American influence on its design make it of 'outstanding national importance'. These are not my words, but are quoted from English Heritage's citation for its Grade II* listing.

London Road (Low Level)

As noted earlier, the GNR diverted virtually all its passenger services from London Road Low Level to the shiny new joint Victoria. A few specials and excursions continued to use Low Level (the Boots outing to Skegness – Chapter 9 – being an example). Otherwise the only passengers that passed through its doors were those using the half dozen or so LNWR trains to and from Northampton. This was due to the fact that the LNWR had failed to gain running powers into Victoria. In fact, Northampton trains continued to use Low Level until 1944, when as a Second World War 'economy measure' these too were diverted into Victoria.

Elsewhere in Nottingham, the LNWR had established a goods station in Manvers Street, and it had built its own eight-road locomotive shed and servicing facilities in the GNR's yard at Colwick.

The sparse passenger traffic using London Road (LL) enabled the GNR to develop its general freight, cattle and parcels traffic into and out of the city. Indeed, until well beyond the age of steam into the mid 1980s it was the hub of BR's Nottingham parcels traffic, eventually handling over a million items per annum.

I cannot conclude this chapter on Nottingham without including this delightful photograph of two, very young, young ladies 'trainspotting' at Nottingham Midland, probably taken around the start of the First World War. The locomotive, no 1345, is one of 200 similar tank locomotives with an 0-4-4 wheel arrangement that were built by the Midland Railway between 1875 and 1900. (Courtesy of Nottingham City Council and Picture the Past)

4

The Midland Spreads Its Wings

Nottingham to Lincoln

For the seven years after the opening of the Midland Counties Railway in 1839, the only 'proper' railway in Nottinghamshire was the branch line from Long Eaton, which terminated in the county town at a station on Carrington Street. That situation began to change in 1846 with the opening of the line from Nottingham to Lincoln. At first glance, linking the two adjacent county towns was a logical move, but the real motive behind the line was not quite as straightforward as it might first seem.

To understand the *raison d'être* for the line we have to turn the clock back two years to 10th May 1844 when the MCR amalgamated with the North Midland and the Birmingham & Derby Junction Railways to form the Midland Railway. The new railway's first chairman was the self styled 'Railway King', George Hudson, who had begun his career working in a York drapery shop. But following a substantial legacy, which he used to indulge in some very dubious wheeling and dealing, by 1844 he found himself in the position of controlling the railway between Rugby and York. Hudson's 'regal' position, however, soon came under threat by the incursion of the proposed London & York Railway – forerunner of part of today's East Coast Main Line – into 'his' kingdom.

Hudson's answer to counter this threat was to build a line from Nottingham to Lincoln, plus a second line connecting Leicester with Peterborough. Rather naively, Hudson believed that by adding these two ancient cathedral cities to the infant Midland Railway's network, he would have a powerful argument to have the London & York Bill rejected by Parliament. That argument was that the L&Y was unnecessary because the MR already linked the two main intermediate cities on its route. But as history has shown, Hudson's objections were dismissed and it does not take a genius to work out why.

Newark's Midland station in BR days after it had acquired the suffix 'Castle' to differentiate it from the GNR station (which became Northgate), with class 2MT 2-6-0 no 46501 heading a Lincoln to Nottingham slow train. Although designed by the LMS, 46501 had been built by BR at the former LNER works at Darlington in 1952, as a stop-gap prior to the introduction of the almost identical BR Standard 78XXX class. Loco 46501 was withdrawn and cut up for scrap in 1967 after a scandalously short life of only 15 years.
(T.G. Hepburn courtesy of the Frank Berridge Collection)

Peterborough to Lincoln is 46½ miles as the crow flies; the rail journey over the Hudson lines via Leicester and Nottingham is 112 miles. Similarly, Peterborough to London by Hudson's route via Leicester and Rugby was 153 miles. Via the subsequent ECML it is exactly half that distance, 76½ miles to be precise.

Such were the 'Punch and Judy' politics of early railway promotion. But at least the Railway King's Nottingham to Lincoln line was not only built, it has survived and is an integral part of the modern cross-country rail network. Although it is outside my geographical terms of reference, exactly the same can be said of the Midland's Leicester to Peterborough line.

But I have digressed …

The Nottingham to Lincoln line's engineer was none other than the great George

Stephenson with whom Hudson was well acquainted. The line probably ranks as one of Stephenson's easiest commissions. It followed the Trent Valley as far as Newark, carefully avoiding the river itself, which it crossed only once. From Newark the route traversed some similarly easy countryside as it passed out of the county into Lincolnshire and on to Lincoln itself. The 32¾ mile long line was constructed in just eight months. Although most are now out of railway use, many of the original station buildings have survived. Several have been listed.

Around the halfway point of the line lies Newark, which was then, and indeed still is, one of Nottinghamshire's more important towns. With numerous maltings, flour mills and several breweries, the new railway immediately opened up new markets for the town's products.

The Southwell branch

Stephenson's Nottingham and Lincoln line bypassed the small, but ecclesiastically important town of Southwell, which is dominated by its magnificent minster. The present building was begun back in 1108 and is one of around only a dozen or so cathedrals in the country on which the title 'minster' has been bestowed.

To keep the natives happy, the Midland opened a short (2½ mile) branch from a junction at Rolleston on the Lincoln line in 1847. It has to be said that in its infancy the branch was not an outstanding success. The initial service of nine trains a day proved to be far too optimistic. The number of daily trains was progressively reduced and in a further desperate attempt to reduce costs, steam was replaced by horsepower. It was a downhill spiral. By 1853 the branch service consisted of a single horse-drawn carriage that ran on Wednesdays only … Wednesday being market day in Newark. Even this was deemed to be uneconomic and was withdrawn. For the next seven years, the rails rusted and any would-be rail passengers had to either use the horse omnibus, or walk the two miles or so to Fiskerton station.

In retrospect, one has to wonder whether George Hudson might perhaps have had an ulterior motive in building the branch. Maybe he hoped that his influence on controlling the railway system between Southwell Minster and the minster in his home city of York might perhaps bring some kind of divine intervention to halt the investigations that had started into his business affairs. It was not to be. The webs of deceit that Hudson had earlier woven in his quest to become the Railway King were untangling at an ever increasing rate. It was eventually revealed that he had regularly lied about the true financial state of his companies. He had bribed Members of Parliament. He had even sold land that he did not own to the nascent Newcastle & Berwick railway company.

The Railway King's fall from grace was spectacular. But perhaps the ultimate irony was that the former Lord Mayor of York was imprisoned for debt for 15 months in

York Castle. Yet his Southwell branch, after its rather inauspicious start, eventually found its place in railway folklore.

Eventually the 'use it or lose it' philosophy seems to have dawned on Southwell's residents. So when passenger services on the branch resumed again in 1860, the patronage was sufficient to ensure continuity (except on Sundays and give or take a few railway strikes) for the next 99 years. Concurrent with the reopening, a new station, Rolleston Junction, was opened where the branch joined the main line.

The train service became known as the 'Southwell Paddy' and took 6 minutes to cover the 2½ miles to the Nottingham–Lincoln line at Rolleston Junction, but only 5 minutes back … or at least that is what the public timetable (perhaps sometimes optimistically) said. (The soubriquet 'Paddy' is a little confusing because, as is explained in the next chapter, the term 'Paddy train' usually referred to the unadvertised workmen's trains that conveyed colliers to and from their pits.)

Some of the 'Paddy' stories have become local legends, such as the train stopping

Southwell railway station photographed in the early years of the last century, with a dozen or so passengers having alighted from the 'Southwell Paddy' wending their way towards the town. On the left can be seen the 'Paddy's' carriages. In the centre is the station building, whilst on the right can be seen part of the goods shed. Hidden behind the goods shed is Southwell's own tiny loco shed, where the branch loco was serviced and stabled overnight. It shared the accommodation with the Newark station pilot – the loco that carried out the shunting duties in and around Newark.
(Courtesy of Nottinghamshire County Council and Picture the Past)

en route if the crew spotted an opportunity to shoot a rabbit, or poach a pheasant or a partridge. Single manning was another trick, particularly during the mellow mists of an autumn morning. The driver would stop the train to allow his fireman to collect wild mushrooms from the lineside fields whilst the train continued to Rolleston with the driver only. On the return journey the train stopped to pick up the fireman and on arrival at Southwell the crew no doubt breakfasted on the mushrooms, together with eggs, bacon and sausage, flash fried in the loco's firebox on the coal shovel.

It has to be said that very similar stories are related about other rural branch lines, from Cornwall to Caithness. But one story, unique to the branch, concerns a Mr Tweedale-Meady, a resident of Southwell. This gentleman was the Clerk to Nottinghamshire County Council in the 1940s and commuted daily by rail from home to County Hall in Nottingham. The first part of his journey was on the 'Paddy' to Rolleston Junction where he changed onto an express to Nottingham. Now I have to admit that the story has probably been embellished over the years, but the gist of it is that one morning the 'Paddy' had left Southwell without Mr Tweedale-Meady on board. It seems that he went ballistic, ***insisting*** not only that the branch train return to pick him up, but that the connecting Nottingham express should be held at Rolleston until he was on board. Such, it seems, was the power of high-ranking civic officials in the age of steam that both demands were met.

Southwell is the birthplace (if 'birth' is the correct horticultural term) of the Bramley apple. The story goes that back in 1809, a young girl by the name of Mary Ann Brailsford planted a few apple pips in a flowerpot. One of the seeds germinated and when it grew too big for the pot Mary Ann transplanted it into the garden of the family's cottage in Easthorpe in Southwell. The property was subsequently bought by Matthew Bramley, a Southwell butcher, who discovered that when Mary Ann's tree reached maturity, the apples were very tart when raw, but when cooked they produced absolutely delicious pies and crumbles.

A local nurseryman named Henry Merryweather got to hear about the quality of the apples and asked for permission to take cuttings from the tree. This permission was granted, but with the proviso that the resulting apples be named 'Bramley Seedlings'. The rest is history except perhaps to say that Mary Ann's tree, which happily still exists, celebrated its 200th anniversary in 2009. One source claims that the fruits from the many descendants of that single seed now account for 95% of all cooking apples sold.

Henry Merryweather sold the first commercially produced Bramley apples in 1862, just as the Southwell railway branch was at last making its mark on the community. Needless to say, over the ensuing years, hundreds, if not thousands, of tons of Bramley apples have begun their journey from the local orchards to the country's markets along the Southwell branch.

The single coach 'Southwell Paddy' at Southwell with former Midland Railway 0-4-4 tank locomotive no 1344 in charge. Both the locomotive and the coach have been modified for 'push-pull' working. When pulling the coach, the driver and fireman travelled together on the loco footplate. When pushing, the driver travelled in a special compartment at the far end of the coach from where he could remotely control the locomotive. The vertical cylinders on the side of the smokebox are part of the remote control gear. (T.G. Hepburn courtesy of the Frank Berridge Collection)

The year 2009 also marked another Southwell anniversary – this time, a sad one – 50 years since the passenger train service was withdrawn. In the 1930s the service became 'push-and-pull' ... the loco pulled the train to Rolleston but pushed it back to Southwell, the driver travelling in a special compartment at the leading end of the passenger coach from where he could see the track and signals ahead and remotely control the locomotive.

On my way to my trainspotting forays at Newark in the late 1950s, recounted in Chapter 8, I can remember seeing the 'Paddy' waiting patiently for passengers at Rolleston Junction. In those days the single coach was usually pushed and pulled by one of the former Midland Railway 0-4-4 tank engines, 58065 and 58085. The pair were amongst the very last survivors of over 200 similar locos that had once been a common sight on Midland and LMS branch lines since Victorian times. Ironically, bearing in mind

The opposite end of the 'Southwell Paddy' photographed at Rolleston Junction. The picture shows the windows that were cut into the end of the coach to enable the driver to see the road ahead when the coach was being propelled. (Courtesy of the Frank Berridge Collection)

that at one time just a single, once a week, horse-powered train had been deemed to be uneconomic, over 40 passenger trains per day were timetabled to travel along the branch at the time of its closure.

The Newark Brake Trials of 1875

Before we leave the Nottingham and Lincoln line and look at the development of the Midland Railway elsewhere in the county, mention must be made of a highly significant series of trials that took place on the line in 1875.

As the early railways developed, so did various forms of train braking systems. These varied from just relying on the handbrakes on the locomotive plus those in one or more brake carriages, through to what was known as a continuous brake. Under normal circumstance the continuous brake, which was controlled by the driver, and which acted on most, if not all, of the carriages, was considerably more efficient.

But there were two basic forms of the continuous brake system. One relied on a pressure or a vacuum or some form of mechanical system to APPLY the brakes along the train. The alternative system used the converse ... that is, pressure or vacuum was necessary to RELEASE the brakes. The **big** advantage of the latter was that it was virtually failsafe. Thus, in the event of a coupling between the carriages breaking and the train becoming divided, the brakes would be automatically applied to **both** sections of the train, which would stop relatively quickly and safely.

By the 1870s most railways were 'doing their own thing' with respect to adopting one of the numerous braking systems that were then available. In an attempt to bring some sort of order to this chaos, a Royal Commission was appointed in 1874 to investigate the problem. Obviously, some practical trials were necessary and the level and reasonably straight section of the Midland's Nottingham and Lincoln line, between Newark and Bleasby, was chosen as the venue.

The trials began on 9th June 1875 and continued (the Sunday excepted) for six days. In addition to the members of the Royal Commission and the Board of Trade's Railway Inspectors, some of the top brass from leading railways from home and abroad were present at the trials. That said, it does appear that the trials were a combination of both a serious fact finding mission, and a 'jolly'. Near to Rolleston Junction station, the Midland Railway had erected a marquee for what in today's parlance would be called 'corporate entertainment'. In charge of this was William Towle, manager of the Midland Hotel in Derby. By this time the Midland was already the 'high flyer' in the world of railway catering. Towle himself was to become a major *tour-de-force* in this field and was knighted in 1920 in recognition of his services.

Six railway companies sent trains, all fitted with different types of brake systems, to take part in the trial. One system – the American-designed Westinghouse Automatic

Air Brake – outclassed the rest by bringing its train to a stand from 51½ mph in 18 seconds having covered a distance of 275 yards. By comparison, trains relying purely on hand-applied brakes on the loco, tender and the guard's brake van needed up to 1,000 yards and took well over a minute to come to a halt from a similar speed. Yet in spite of its superiority, the Westinghouse system was not greeted with universal enthusiasm for use in the UK. Part of the problem was that the loco needed to be fitted with an auxiliary air compressor, which the loco engineers of the day considered as additional equipment to maintain and to go wrong.

The train fitted with the automatic vacuum brake also acquitted itself well and thus it was, with a few exceptions, that the vacuum brake became the standard on UK railways in the days of steam.

But amazingly it took until 1889 before automatic brakes became a mandatory requirement for passenger trains in the UK. It was the public backlash following a horrendous accident at Armagh in Northern Ireland that killed 78 people – many of them children returning from a Sunday School outing – that finally spurred Parliament into action. This accident, which at the time was the worst, not only in the UK but in the whole of Europe, was due primarily to the carriages not being fitted with efficient automatic brakes.

The Erewash Valley

Hard on the heels of the opening of the Southwell branch came the long awaited arrival of a railway into the Erewash Valley.

During the first three decades of the 19th century, the majority of the smoke emanating from the domestic and industrial chimneys of the East Midlands, and beyond, was from the burning of Erewash coal. But as we saw in Chapter 1, the monopoly of Erewash coal sales in Leicester was shattered by the opening of the Leicester & Swannington Railway in 1832 and the coalmasters' scheme to promote their own railway was hi-jacked. But it was not until 1847 that the Midland Railway (the Midland Counties Railway's successor) opened the first part of its Erewash Valley branch, the 12 miles from Long Eaton to Codnor Park. Here the attraction was the Butterley Company's thriving ironworks with its connections to that company's own extensive railway system, which linked many of its collieries and its foundries.

In 1851 the Erewash line was extended northward to Pinxton and thence to Kirkby over the newly upgraded Mansfield & Pinxton Railway line. At Kirkby a connection was made to the Nottingham–Mansfield line (see below).

The Leen Valley

It could be argued that Mansfield first appeared on the railway maps of Great Britain as early as 1819 with the opening of the 4' 4" gauge horse-drawn tramway from

Pinxton. But it took a further 30 years before it was finally connected to the ever expanding standard gauge network on 10th October 1849.

This was via the Midland Railway's line from Nottingham along the Leen Valley.

The River Leen rises in the Robin Hood Hills near Kirkby-in-Ashfield and flows in a generally southern direction to Nottingham where it joins the River Trent. From early medieval times the Leen's waters had been harnessed to provide power for the numerous mills built alongside its course. Initially these were flour mills, but eventually many were converted to process cotton. Yet in spite of the pockets of industry dotted along the river's banks, the valley on either side was largely rural in nature. For the Midland Railway, the valley provided the easiest and most direct route to Mansfield. But the line proved to be the catalyst that transformed the previously mainly pastoral valley into a corridor of collieries.

The line opened in two stages. The first section, just over 12 miles in length, from Nottingham to Kirkby, opened on 2nd October 1848, which happened to coincide with the annual Goose Fair. Naturally the latter ensured plenty of patronage initially, but the local press was far from enthusiastic about the long-term future as it considered charging 4d for the 2¼ mile journey in an open, third class carriage from Radford to Nottingham to be excessive. The second section, the four miles from Kirkby into Mansfield, opened, as noted above, just over a year later on 10th October 1849. Much of the latter was over a section of the upgraded former Mansfield and Pinxton line.

In 1861 the shafts for Hucknall No 1 Colliery were sunk in the Leen Valley. It was the tip of the iceberg. Hucknall No 2 soon followed and in the ensuing years mines at Annesley, Bestwood, Linby, Newstead and Radford were opened. Inevitably these collieries were soon connected to MR's Leen Valley line.

But as we shall see in later chapters, both the Great Northern and the Manchester, Sheffield & Lincolnshire Railway Companies were casting covetous eyes on the Leen Valley.

Chronologically, before the MR reached Mansfield, the MS&LR had established a foothold in the north of the county with the opening of its Sheffield to Gainsborough line in July 1849, which put both Worksop and Retford on the railway map.

Southwell to Mansfield

As we saw earlier, Southwell found itself on the railway map in 1847, but for the first 13 years of its history, the little branch line from Rolleston Junction had a rather chequered career. It took until 1860 for the service to really establish itself. The Midland had plans to extend the branch to Mansfield through the heart of Sherwood Forest where some of Robin Hood's exploits are alleged to have taken place. Maid Marion is reputed to have lived at Blidworth, and the locals claim that Will Scarlet is

Super power in the form of two former LMS 8F 2-8-0s, nos 48100 and 48528, heading away from Mansfield Crown Farm on a bright January day in 1959. On the left on the horizon is the easily recognisable outline of the building housing the colliery's washery. On the right is the colliery spoil heap, which was affectionately known by the locals as 'Mount Crownie'.
(Courtesy of the Frank Berridge Collection)

buried in Blidworth churchyard. Nearby is Fountain Dale where Robin is supposed to have first encountered Friar Tuck.

The less than impressive early performance of the Southwell branch was probably the reason for the Midland's reticence to continue the line to Mansfield. But then a Southwell businessman jerked the MR into action by threatening to build the line himself.

It may have been a bluff, but the Midland's response was the 12½ mile line that opened in April 1871. Most of it was single track with just one passing loop at Farnsfield, which was around the midway point. The Newark to Mansfield passenger service over the line was dire. Whilst the pace of life was generally a lot slower in Victorian and Edwardian times, taking around an hour for the 18½ mile journey with only five intermediate stops was a joke.

In later years the opening of new collieries at Mansfield Crown Farm (1905), Rufford (1915), Clipstone (1922) and Blidworth (1926) eventually brought some degree of prosperity to the line. Even further into the future, the joint LMS/LNER Mid Notts Railway (Chapter 7), which served Bilsthorpe and Ollerton Collieries, connected with the Southwell and Mansfield near Farnsfield.

Mansfield to Worksop

Having arrived in Mansfield, the Midland began looking at extending its influence north towards Worksop where, as noted above, the MS&LR already had a firm foothold. The first proposal was abandoned due to opposition from the ducal landowners *en route*, but a second attempt was more successful, His Grace the Duke of Portland even paying for one of the stations (Whitwell).

Although both Mansfield and Worksop are in Nottinghamshire, the majority of the line between the two lies on the Derbyshire side of the county boundary. The only intermediate station in Notts was that at Mansfield Woodhouse. Oddly, perhaps reflecting the station's name, this was constructed of timber whereas the remainder of the stations were somewhat more substantially built in the local magnesian limestone.

With Mansfield having become the terminus of trains from Nottingham, Pye Bridge (on the Erewash Valley line) and more recently from Newark and Southwell, the Midland decided to provide a better station in the town. This would be even more vital when the new Worksop line opened.

The new Italianate style station opened in April 1872, beyond which was (and still is) the 15 span brick and masonry viaduct. Travelling over this, rail passengers to and from Worksop got a bird's-eye view of the heart of the town.

The northern end of the line formed a triangular junction with the MS&LR between Shireoaks and Worksop. The eastern leg of the triangle allowed Midland trains into Worksop station whilst the western leg was used by the MS&LR's Sheffield to Mansfield service under reciprocal running powers.

The 'Penny Emma'

Before moving away from the Mansfield area, mention must be made of the Midland's short branch to Sutton-in-Ashfield, the trains on which were universally known by the town's inhabitants as the 'Penny Emma'. Until the branch opened on 1st May 1893 the town's only station was on the MR Leen Valley line, a good mile away from the centre. It was the threat of the Great Northern building a much more convenient station in Sutton on its Leen Valley Extension that galvanised the Midland into action. The result was a ¾ mile long line from the original Sutton station, which was then renamed Sutton Junction.

The origin of the name 'Penny Emma' is a matter of debate. The 'Penny' element is straightforward as that was the cost of a ticket to the main line at Sutton Junction. Where 'Emma' comes from is somewhat more obscure. Some claim that it was the name of the branch locomotive, but this is rather unlikely as the Midland was very frugal in bestowing names on its engines. Certainly this did not include the ubiquitous 0-4-4 tank engines that shuffled to and fro along the branch.

The theory that I subscribe to is that 'Emma' is a local dialect corruption of the letters 'M R' to differentiate it from the services to and from Sutton provided by the

A view of the Midland Railway's station at Sutton-in-Ashfield at the end of the ¾ mile branch from Sutton Junction. Judging by the style of clothes being worn by the two ladies who have brought the infants in their care to 'look at the trains', the photograph was taken circa 1910.
(Courtesy A.P. Knighton and Picture the Past)

GNR and, later, the GCR. But whatever its origins 'a trip on t'train t'junction 'n' back' was a simple and inexpensive treat for many Sutton townsfolk.

Except for the building of the third Nottingham Midland station on Carrington Street (Chapter 3), the Sutton branch was the last significant MR development in Nottinghamshire. But predating both these were the Radford and Trowell, and the Nottingham and Melton lines.

The five mile long Radford and Trowell line, opened in 1875, provided a by-pass between the Leen and Erewash Valley lines that enabled through passenger and freight traffic to avoid the congestion around the Toton marshalling yards. By avoiding Toton the distance between Trowell to Nottingham was reduced by four miles. No passenger stations were provided, but *en route* connections were made to the collieries at Wollaton and Trowell.

It was the penultimate piece of the jigsaw. The final part of the plan was a direct line from Nottingham to Kettering via Melton Mowbray, which would at last put Nottingham on a through route from London to the north.

The original seeds had been sown when the Great Northern and London & North Western Railways began plotting to get a slice of the iron ore traffic emanating from Leicestershire and Northamptonshire. The Midland's line from Leicester to Peterborough, built in 1848 by George Hudson, ran nominally west to east across the area. After a little deliberation, the Midland decided to counter the GNR/LNWR threat by building a 17½ mile line from London Road Junction just east of Nottingham station to join Hudson's line near Melton Mowbray. Although it is outside the geographical boundaries of this volume, London bound trains then continued towards Peterborough for 16 miles before branching off at Manton towards Corby and Kettering. Although intermediate stations were provided, local traffic seemed not to be actively encouraged so that the line would be kept relatively clear for through freight and express passenger services.

Freight services began in 1879 and on 1st March 1882 express trains started using the line. Distance-wise, the difference between the two St Pancras to Nottingham routes was negligible; the one via Melton was just a mile shorter.

From then on, the Midland's expresses from London to Leeds and Bradford, or beyond, over the Settle and Carlisle line to Scotland were generally routed via Melton Mowbray, Nottingham and the Erewash Valley. London to Manchester trains normally travelled via Leicester and Derby.

One interesting little aside is that in 1946, the 10.00 am from London St Pancras to Glasgow St Enoch via Melton Mowbray, Nottingham ***and*** Derby gained the dubious distinction of travelling through more tunnels on its journey than any other British train. In aggregate, the train was underground for around 15 miles as it passed through no fewer than 40 different tunnels. Of these, only one was in Nottinghamshire –

the 1,330 yard long Stanton Tunnel, which lies between Widmerpool and Plumtree. Incidentally this tunnel was (and still is) the longest tunnel in the county.

A London St Pancras bound express roaring through the long closed and deserted Plumtree station on 5th November 1956. The motive power for the train is being provided by one of the mixed traffic 4-6-0 locos, which were known universally as 'Black Fives'. Many expresses on the Midland main line at the time were hauled by the slightly larger and more powerful Jubilee class locomotives, which were all named. In LMS days the Jubilees carried the distinctive crimson lake (maroon) livery; in BR days this was changed to mid Brunswick green. By contrast the Black Fives remained black throughout their lives, but although not as glamorous and smaller and less powerful than the Jubilees, they were very popular locomotives with footplate crews. Not only were they very free steaming, when the chips were down a Black Five could produce a performance that in theory was way beyond its capabilities. (Photo by Henry Priestley, courtesy of Nottinghamshire County Council and Picture the Past)

5

A Cuckoo in the Nest

As we saw in Chapter 3, the initially independent Ambergate, Nottingham, Boston & Eastern Junction Railway had built a line between Grantham and Colwick, which opened in July 1850. The final two or three miles from Colwick into Nottingham were by courtesy of running powers over Midland Railway metals. This ambivalence by the MR was because it believed that the ANB&EJR would become part of its own empire. But as history has shown, the Midland was in fact allowing a cuckoo, in the guise of the Great Northern Railway, into its nest.

The major civil engineering project on the Nottinghamshire section of the ANB&EJR was the crossing of the River Trent and its flood plain near Radcliffe. The river bridge, which is still in use today, consists of an elegant segmentally arched iron girder span followed by three masonry arches. The flood plain was originally traversed by a wooden viaduct, but this was replaced in 1910 by a brick viaduct.

As we also saw in Chapter 3, in spite of its grand aspirations, the ANB&EJR got no further west than Nottingham or further east than Grantham. For the first two years of its existence the line was worked by a private contractor, E.B. Wilson & Co of Leeds. But this was to change with the opening of the Great Northern's so called 'Towns Line' from Peterborough to Doncaster in 1852. From being merely at the end of a branch line from Nottingham, Grantham now found itself on what subsequently became part of the East Coast Main Line – 30 miles of which, as we will see in Chapter 8, runs through the east of the county.

With one of the ANB&EJR's major shareholders also being a director of the Great Northern, it was inevitable that a connection between the two lines was made at Grantham. Subsequently the GNR took over the operation of the Nottingham line from Wilson's. For the GNR, the ANB&EJR was a heaven sent opportunity to strike at the heart of the ever expanding Midland Railway empire.

Having eventually established its own handsome terminus in Nottingham, the

This is an obviously posed shot of the down (towards Nottingham) platform at Aslockton station on the ANB&EJR line, taken circa 1920. In the centre and on the right are two of the station's porters with milk churns, which were once a familiar sight on every rural station platform. Standing smartly to attention between the porters, with a white hanky in his breast pocket is the Station Master, who in those days was a highly respected member of the community. What appears to be a grandfather clock towards the left hand side of the photograph is actually a penny-in-the-slot personal weighing machine, which at the time was one of the few ways of checking your weight … albeit when fully dressed. Some of the more advanced versions actually printed your weight on a ticket. The building behind is branded as the 'General Waiting Room'. It was equipped with a stove to keep the waiting passengers warm in the winter, but was available for use by both 1st and 2nd class passengers of both sexes. Many stations also had 'Ladies Waiting Rooms' where not only could women escape from predatory males, they provided facilities for nursing mothers to feed their babies in private.
(Courtesy of Nottinghamshire County Council and Picture the Past)

GNR began casting covetous eyes on the ever increasing coal traffic emanating from the collieries in the Leen and Erewash valleys where the Midland held the monopoly. Perhaps equally tempting would be the political coup that the GNR would achieve by extending their line through the Midland's heartland in Derby and on to Burton-on-Trent to tap into another lucrative source of income … the brewery traffic generated in the town.

The eventual result was the GNR's Derbyshire & Staffordshire Lines Act, which after being approved by Parliament was granted Royal Assent in June 1872. The Act also included the branch up the Erewash Valley to Pinxton.

The Derbyshire lines began from a triangular junction with the ANB&EJR at Colwick where the GNR would build an extensive marshalling yard and loco shed. The triangular junctions allowed through running in both directions from the ANB&EJR.

It was a difficult line to construct and subsequently to work. From Colwick the line began by climbing for 3 miles, mostly at 1 in 100, through Gedling and the 1,132 yard long Mapperley Tunnel to the summit at Arno Vale. From the summit the line descended on a variety of gradients for 2½ miles through Daybrook to Basford & Bulwell, where some local passenger services terminated. Trains continuing towards Derby (or Pinxton) then faced another stiff 1 in 100 climb, this time slightly shorter at 2½ miles, to Kimberley. But to reach Kimberley the GNR's contractor had to quarry through over two miles of hard magnesian limestone interspersed with strata of shale. The resulting cutting, in places, was over 50 feet deep. The ingress of water

Bennerley Viaduct photographed during the latter stages of construction in 1877. It was 1,452 feet in length and carried the Great Northern Railway's Derbyshire Extension lines 60 feet above the Erewash Valley. (Courtesy of Derbyshire Local Studies Libraries and Picture the Past)

gave the contractor (the experienced Benton & Woodisse & Co) headaches that approached severe migraine proportions.

The cutting was punctuated by the relatively short, 268 yard Watnall Tunnel, the boring of which was even more problematical due to water. Indeed, to get the line open and avoid the financial penalties that would have been imposed by Parliament if the line was not opened in the specified time, the GNR constructed a 1 in 30 avoiding line over the tunnel. The eastern part of this temporary avoiding line subsequently became part of the GNR's connection with the Barber, Walker & Co colliery network.

At Kimberley, further quarrying was required to accommodate the goods yard.

A class J6 0-6-0 bustles into the former GNR station at Kimberley ... later renamed Kimberley East to differentiate it from the former Midland Railway's premises, which became Kimberley West. After leaving Kimberley the train will either head along the main line to Ilkeston and Derby or turn off onto the Pinxton branch at Awsworth Junction, which was just over half-a-mile beyond the station. The rather grandiose station nameboard on the left of the photograph reads 'Kimberley for Watnall, Nuthall and Giltbrook', below which was added 'Change for Pinxton and Derby Trains'. The footbridge not only provided safe access between the platforms, it was extended to maintain the public footpath between Chapel Street and Rock Side. Although the bridge in the photograph has long gone, it has been replaced by a high level walkway spanning the former station site.
(Courtesy A.P. Knighton and Picture the Past)

On the plus side, the limestone quarried provided a ready source of raw material for building bridges and other structures. For instance, at Kimberley the Nottingham turnpike had to be lowered to allow sufficient clearance for traffic to pass beneath the GNR's overbridge. The still extant walls of resulting 'road cutting' on Main Street are lined with magnesian limestone excavated nearby by Benton & Woodisse's navvies.

From Kimberley, westbound trains could coast downhill for the next two miles through Awsworth to the major engineering work on the Derbyshire Extension lines … the magnificent Bennerley Viaduct. On this structure, the GNR's trains strode boldly across the Erewash Valley and on into Derbyshire.

The choice of a lattice wrought iron structure was due to the unstable and unpredictable nature of the ground after years of unrecorded coal mining activities. Compared to the foundation loads that would have been imposed by a conventional masonry viaduct, the wrought iron lattice structure was significantly lighter and therefore more stable. It was to prove to be a wise decision. Indeed, Bennerley Viaduct has led a rather charmed life.

As an example, on 31st January 1916, a hopelessly lost German Zeppelin (the L20) mistook Ilkeston and the nearby Stanton Ironworks for Liverpool (its intended target). Several of the Zeppelin's bombs fell close to Bennerley Viaduct, but the resulting blast waves passed harmlessly through the open lattice structure, which emerged from the raid unscathed.

The last train rumbled over the viaduct in 1968, but as we will see in Chapter 12, its charmed life has not only ensured that it survived into the 21st century, its significance has been recognised by it now being listed as a Grade II* structure.

The Pinxton branch

The GNR's assault to break the Midland's monopoly in the Notts & Derby coalfield began with the 7¾ mile long branch line which ran from a junction between Kimberley and Awsworth through the Erewash Valley to Pinxton.

The start of the branch over what the locals called the '40 Bridges' was spectacular. In official circles it was known as both Awsworth Viaduct and Giltbrook Viaduct. The sinuously curved structure, which measured 1,716 feet in length, actually comprised 43 rather than 40 spans, constructed from locally made bricks. Two of the spans were bricked up to provide living accommodation for the brickies and navvies working on the line.

The first coal trains began running over '40 Bridges' and the Erewash Valley in August 1875, some two and a half years before Bennerley Viaduct and the line into Derbyshire opened for business. The arrival of the GNR and the breaking of the Midland's monopoly were generally greeted with enthusiasm by the colliery owners who could now play one line off against the other in order to achieve the most favourable rates. Passenger services on the branch began some 12 months later, in August 1876.

In addition to the '40 Bridges' there was another lengthy brick viaduct on the Pinxton branch, this time at Jacksdale. Although considerably shorter than '40 Bridges' – it actually only consisted of 20 spans – there were station platforms on the top of the structure with the booking office etc housed underneath the arches. Although situated in the village of Jacksdale, it was one of those stations where the railway authorities didn't seem to be really sure of its location. Originally named Codnor Park & Selston, the Selston appendage was removed in 1901. Subsequently 'for Ironville and Jacksdale' were added to Codnor Park. It took the nationalised British Railways to right all the previous wrongs by correctly naming the station Jacksdale.

But irrespective of the station's name, waiting for a train on the exposed platforms atop of a windswept viaduct in inclement weather cannot have been a pleasant experience. Nevertheless, passenger services on the branch as a whole continued until January 1963.

At the terminus at Pinxton, the layout and the operation of passenger services were somewhat curious to say the least.

Normally, a country branch line terminus had a single platform with what is known in the trade as a 'run-round loop'. After arriving at the terminus, the locomotive would uncouple from its train and use the run-round loop to run past the train before coupling onto what had previously been the rear of the train and then returning from whence it came along the branch. It was (and still is on many heritage railways) a simple and straightforward procedure.

But at Pinxton there was an arrival platform and **two** departure platforms. The latter were on an island, devoid of any form of shelter, staggered completely from the arrival platform and the station buildings – see the simplified sketch plan of the track layout.

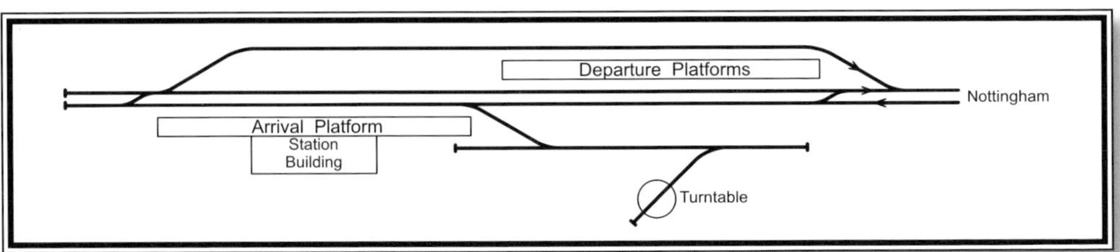

On the arrival of a passenger train at Pinxton, the locomotive, which invariably would be travelling chimney first, uncoupled and began to run round the coaches. In the meantime, the platform staff would be busy unloading inbound parcels and other goods from the guard's van, whilst at the same time loading outbound parcels and goods. Having completed running round (and hopefully the staff having completed the station work), the locomotive then shunted the train across to one of the departure platforms. At some point in the proceedings, logically during the run round, the locomotive was rotated through 180° on the turntable so that it would return to Nottingham (and sometimes to destinations further afield) with the chimney leading. This was an operational requirement instituted back in early GNR days after a Nottingham bound train running bunker first was involved in a fatal accident. That said, towards the end of the branch's life (it closed in January 1963), the turntable had long been out of use. In the early 1950s the 'inner face' of the island platform was made redundant and later in the decade the remains of the departure platform were removed completely.

The Leen Valley

Having given the Midland a 'bloody nose' in the Erewash Valley the GNR decided to flex its muscles further and challenge the MR's monopoly in the Leen Valley.

Apart from a short section near Pye Hill (GNR) and Pye Bridge (MR) the two Erewash Valley lines kept a respectable distance from each other. But in the Leen Valley they ran 'cheek by jowl', crossing and recrossing each other several times.

Beginning at the appropriately named Leen Valley Junction, one mile west of Daybrook station, the line, which opened for business on 1st October 1882, ran for some 7 miles to Annesley. The Midland, being first on the scene, had obviously chosen the easiest route for its line. The GNR had to be content with second best.

At the northern end of the Leen Valley is a sandstone ridge known as the Robin Hood Hills. The Midland, *en route* to Mansfield had penetrated the ridge with the relatively short (199 yard long) Kirkby Tunnel. But having broken the Midland's monopoly of the Leen Valley collieries, the GNR decide to call it a day because they considered that tunnelling under the hills was not a worthwhile enterprise. That, however, was not a view that was shared by the Manchester, Sheffield & Lincolnshire Railway.

Now, I called this chapter 'Cuckoo in the nest' because of the Midland's naivety in allowing the GNR in the form of the ANB&EJR to invade its territory. But the GNR in building its Leen Valley line was effectively building a nest for another, even more invasive cuckoo to lay its eggs. That cuckoo, as we shall see in Chapter 6, was the Manchester, Sheffield & Lincolnshire Railway.

The MS&LR, which up to this point was a successful west to east railway, began casting covetous eyes southward, initially towards obtaining access to the Nottinghamshire coalfield. The GNR's Leen Valley line was ripe for the plucking.

The initial approach was fairly innocuous. The MS&LR would build a 'branch'

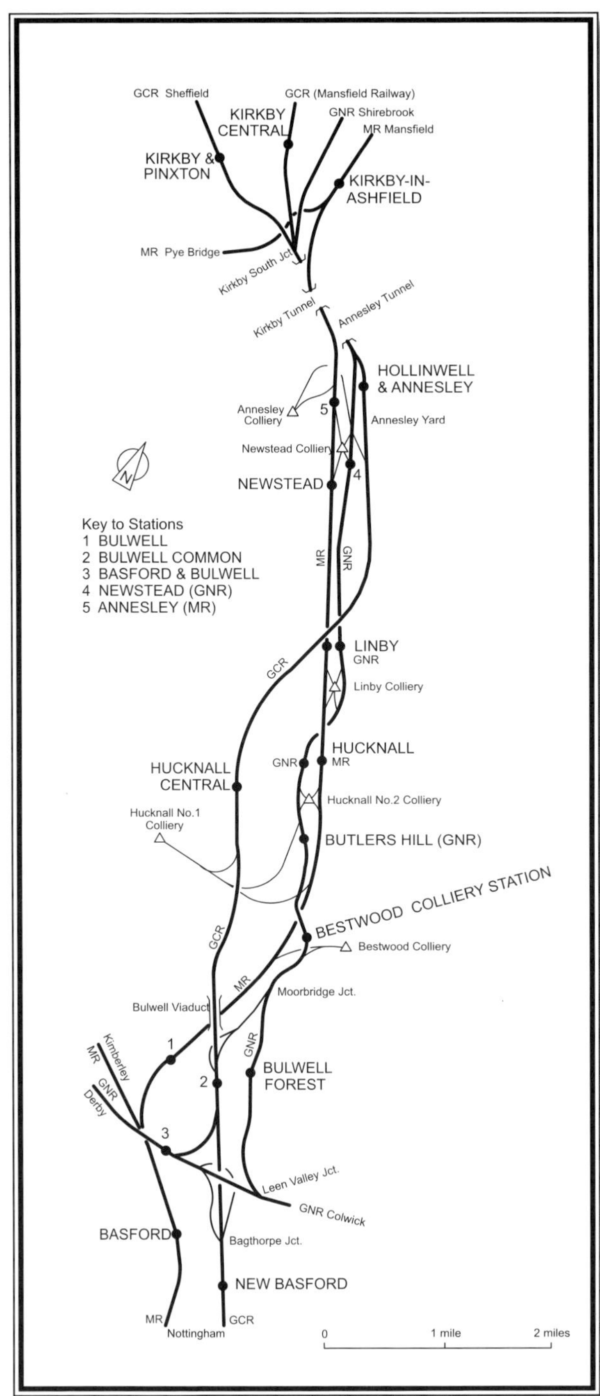

(albeit some 24 miles in length) from their main line at Beighton on the Yorkshire/Derbyshire border east of Sheffield to make an 'end-on' connection with the GNR Leen Valley line at Annesley. This of course would involve boring through the Robin Hood Hills. The resulting tunnel was 1,001 yards in length.

Rather naively the GNR agreed to support the scheme. In return for running powers over the MS&LR into Sheffield (Victoria), the GNR allowed the MS&LR running powers over the Leen Valley line (including the collieries) and into Nottingham (London Road). The MS&LR was cock-a-hoop. It had a ready-made export market for Notts coal through its North Sea ports at Immingham and Grimsby. But more importantly, although unstated at the time, the Annesley branch was to provide the take off point for the MS&LR's king-size cuckoo, the audacious London Extension (see Chapter 6).

A map of the Leen Valley's railways after the opening of the Great Central (Chapter 6) showing the connections that it made with the GNR and the connections the railways built to serve the Leen Valley collieries.

Class O4 2-8-0 no 63751 passing the platforms of Skegby and Stanton Hill station on the GNR Leen Valley Extension line with a train of empty mineral wagons for one of the local collieries in July 1955. This locomotive had begun life in 1917 as ROD no 1833, becoming war surplus after the cessation of hostilities. It was eventually bought by the LNER in 1927 for the princely sum of £340, was renumbered LNER 6574, and stayed in the UK for the duration of the Second World War, although 92 of these rugged, reliable machines were requisitioned and used on a supply route from Persia to Russia. It became BR no 63751 in 1948 and was finally withdrawn in 1959. (H.B. Priestley/ Picture the Past)

On the same day that Henry Priestley photographed 63751 at Skegby, his camera captured another 2-8-0 war veteran, now carrying the BR no 90000, heading in the opposite direction with a loaded coal train.
Introduced in 1943, a total of 935 of these so called Austerity locomotives were built in just under two and a half years for service during the war; 545 were built at the North British Locomotive Co works in Glasgow, the remainder by the Vulcan Foundry of Newton-le-Willows. After the war, 200 were purchased by the LNER and following nationalisation a further 533 were acquired by British Railways. Over 200 of the same class were bought by the Dutch Railways. (H.B. Priestley/ Picture the Past)

The Leen Valley Extension

The first MS&LR freight trains began to appear at Annesley in October 1892. MS&LR passenger services to Nottingham London Road commenced at the beginning of January 1893.

With the opening of the MS&LR's Annesley Tunnel and its running powers through it, the GNR could now look beyond the Leen Valley to challenge the Midland's monopoly of the collieries beyond the Robin Hood Hills. It was a challenge that was particularly encouraged by the Stanton Iron Co, who owned mines at Teversall, Pleasley and Silverhill.

The extension began at what became known as Kirkby South Junction, half-a-mile or so north of Annesley Tunnel. At this point the MS&LR line was in a deep cutting (see photograph on page 72). The line, eventually 9¾ miles in length, opened piecemeal, the first section to Silverhill Colliery in February 1897. Passenger services through Sutton-in-Ashfield to Skegby began the following year. Shirebrook Colliery became connected to the GNR system in 1900 and a year later the passenger service was extended to Shirebrook and on to Langwith Junction on the Lancashire, Derbyshire & East Coast Railway's main line between Chesterfield and Lincoln.

On the branch line from just north of Skegby to serve the Silverhill and Teversall collieries, the GNR built a substantial passenger station, which had all the usual facilities, to serve the village of Teversall. Yet except for the occasional summer seaside excursion trains, it was hardly ever used by the general public. That said, it did see many passengers – miners – who travelled to and from work on unadvertised 'Paddy trains'. (The derivation of the name 'Paddy trains' can be traced back to the early days of railway construction when the navvies, many of them originating from the Emerald Isle, were taken to the various work sites, in crude, open wagons.)

In the days before pit-head baths, miners had to travel to and from work in their dirty clothes. But travelling on ordinary passenger trains in 'dirties' was not an option as it was illegal. An updated form of Paddy train provided the answer. Consisting of long superannuated carriages, these trains, which did not appear in public timetables, carried miners to and from the pits. It was custom and practice for every miner to have his own seat, on which, after arrival at the mine, he could safely leave his pipe, tobacco, cigarettes, matches and anything else that was strictly forbidden to be taken underground, knowing that his possessions would still be there on his seat at the end of the shift. Paddy trains continued to operate after the advent of pit-head baths to provide miners with a convenient and reliable means of travelling to and from work.

Regular passenger services from Skegby were withdrawn in 1931, but the station remained open into the 1960s for the unadvertised Paddy trains and the occasional excursion. Local legend has it that, ironically, it was one of these excursions that saw the final demise of the station. Whilst waiting for one of these trains, a young lady who was wearing stiletto heel shoes broke a heel in the gaps between the wooded platform planking and sued BR. Rather than risk similar litigation in future BR decided to call it a day, and close the station.

The Great Northern and London & North Western joint line

In addition to the collieries to the north and west of Nottingham, the ironstone mines to the south in Leicestershire and Northamptonshire also proved to have a magnetic attraction for the GNR.

Whilst still foraging westwards with their Derbyshire and Staffordshire Extension lines, the GNR management were planning new conquests by building a new line from just south of Newark, through Nottinghamshire to Melton Mowbray and on into Leicester itself, picking up business from the ironstone mines it encountered *en route*.

The first section, the nine miles from the ECML at Newark to the ANB&EJR line at Bottesford was pretty straightforward and there were no major engineering obstacles to overcome. Only one station was provided, which was named Cotham. In reality it was not a good investment. The station was situated a good mile away from the tiny village of the same name. With a total population of around 100, passenger revenues were always minimal. Goods traffic along the line began in April 1878 with the first passenger trains between Nottingham and Newark commencing a year later. Having arrived at Bottesford, where there was a single junction facing towards Nottingham, the GNR's plans seem to have run out of steam … or more accurately, to have run out of money.

Bottesford lies just over the border in Leicestershire, as does the rest of the route of the GNR's proposed ironstone line through that county, so in theory the rest of the story is outside my Nottinghamshire Railway brief. Suffice to say here therefore that waiting and watching from the wings was the London & North Western Railway, who could see that a coalition with the GNR to continue the ironstone line would be to the benefit of both companies.

Thus a joint GNR/LNWR line from Bottesford to Medbourne on the LNWR's route from Market Harborough to Peterborough came to fruition. Inevitably, the LNWR drove a hard bargain. This included running powers over a number of Nottinghamshire GNR lines and even into Nottingham itself where LNWR passenger trains to and from Northampton used London Road station. Nearby, the LNWR established its own comprehensive goods station in Manvers Street.

One section of GNR/LNWR joint line was built in Nottinghamshire. To relieve congestion on the ANB&EJR, a short cut was constructed from Saxondale through Bingham and Barnstone to Stathern Junction on the main part of the joint line.

6

The Last Main Line

The social repercussions of the arrival and the development of railways throughout all parts of the country were enormous. But few approached the upheaval that was caused by the construction of the Manchester, Sheffield & Lincolnshire Railway's London Extension through Nottinghamshire and beyond in the closing decade of the 19th century.

As we will see, Nottingham was particularly affected.

The MS&LR London Extension was, until the building of the Channel Tunnel Rail Link (otherwise known as 'High Speed One') over 100 years later, the last main line to be built in Britain. Yet interestingly, or ironically, depending on your point of view, both the MS&LR London Extension and High Speed One, as we shall see later, have a common denominator.

To understand the story, we need to turn the clock back to 1845 and the opening of the Sheffield, Ashton-under-Lyne & Manchester Railway. To achieve its objective of connecting Manchester with Sheffield, the line had to burrow for over three miles beneath the Woodhead Moors. At the time of opening, the Woodhead Tunnel was the country's, if not the world's, longest railway tunnel. But having arrived in Sheffield, the SA&MR was courted by and eventually amalgamated with two companies anxious to connect the City of Steel with Lincolnshire and the east coast. Most of the story of these lines is outside the geographical scope of this narrative, other than to say that the SA&MR changed its name to Manchester, Sheffield & Lincolnshire Railway at the beginning of 1847. Rather more relevant is that the new main line from Sheffield towards Lincolnshire, which opened in July 1849, put the north Notts towns of Worksop and Retford on the railway map.

The MS&LR eventually served many Lincolnshire towns and villages and was responsible for the development of the port facilities at Grimsby and Immingham. And through being a partner (along with the Midland and the Great Northern) in the Cheshire Lines Committee, it also reached the west coast, the 'jewel in the crown' being Liverpool. The bottom line to this was that as the 19th century began to draw to a close, the MS&LR together with its 1/3 share in the CLC made it essentially just an west to east railway. That said, it was a very successful one.

Edward Watkin

No essay on the MS&LR can ignore the influence of the remarkable Sir Edward William Watkin, Bart, on the fortunes of the company.

At the age of 11, the young Edward Watkin was present at the opening of the world's first inter-city line, the Liverpool & Manchester Railway. Bearing in mind his future railway career, the event must have been a defining moment in the young boy's life.

Born in 1819, Watkin was the son of a successful Manchester cotton merchant. But after a privileged education, he turned his back on the family business and at the age of 26 became the Secretary of the Trent Valley Railway. A few months later, the Trent Valley became part of the London & North Western Railway. Watkin's undoubted managerial talents were quickly recognised and he soon found himself as the assistant to the LNWR's General Manager, Captain Mark Huish.

Huish's rather cavalier style of management and, if I may say it, some of his dubious business ethics no doubt had some influence on Watkin's later career. But Mark Huish was a dynamic leader. Exactly the same can be said about Edward Watkin.

Watkin left the LNWR in 1854 to become the General Manager of the MS&LR, a post that he held for 8 years. Two years later, in 1864, he was appointed Chairman of the MS&LR, in which position he reigned supreme for 30 years. His eventual CV was almost unbelievable. Space precludes a complete résumé, but in addition to his multifarious railway interests, Watkin was also an MP. He represented Great Yarmouth briefly in 1857–1858. Six years later he was back at Westminster as Stockport's MP from 1864 to 1868. After another 6 year break he did a final 21 year stint in Parliament from 1874 to 1895 as the MP for Hythe in Kent. Although born in Salford and consequently having northern roots, he seems to have had a strong affinity to the south, and beyond. He was a director of the Great Western Railway, the Great Eastern Railway and also, and perhaps more significantly, he was a member of the board of the Chemin de Fer du Nord in France, the railway that connected Paris with northern French cities and ports. Add into this already complex equation Watkin's chairmanship of the South Eastern Railway, which included routes between London and the Channel Ports, and his position as Chairman of the Metropolitan Railway, which stretched northward from London into Buckinghamshire, and the scene is set …

For Watkin, there were two rather large 'gaps' in his empire.

One was the lack of a Watkin controlled line between leafy Buckinghamshire and the polluted industrial heartlands of south Yorkshire. The other was a rail link between the English Channel ports served by his SER and Calais or Boulogne, which were served by the Nord Railway in France.

The latter problem Watkin attempted to solve by his deep involvement with a proposal to build a Channel Tunnel. Initially the scheme had a lot of support, including Queen Victoria's consort, Prince Albert. Indeed, in 1880, trial tunnels were begun on both sides of the Channel. Even the Prime Minister, William Ewart Gladstone, inspected progress.

By 1883, both these headings were over a mile in length. But the British Government suddenly panicked and forbade any further work to take place because of fears that a tunnel could be used by foreign armies to invade our island stronghold. In the light of the invasion of France by the Nazis in 1940, it was perhaps in retrospect a very wise decision. That said, right from the start of the project, the War Office had insisted that gunpowder charges would need to be placed at regular intervals through the completed tunnel. These would be detonated in the event of a hostile undersea invasion. But one has to seriously question the safety implications for ordinary trains passing through the tunnel legitimately!

Undeterred by this setback, Watkin still pressed ahead with his second scheme, which was to transform his MS&LR into a vital component of his 'Grand Plan' to invade Europe. The result was the MS&LR's London Extension. Its effect on Nottingham, in particular, was profound.

Whilst, officially, the initials MS&L stand for the 'Manchester, Sheffield and Lincolnshire', contemporary cynics claimed that more accurately, MS&L stood for 'Money Sunk and Lost'. The name change to the Great Central Railway that occurred in 1897 to reflect the railway's new role did little to stem the controversy. For the devout believers, GCR stood for God's Chosen Railway, whilst for the cynics GC meant that their money had Gone Completely.

Both camps could claim a degree of credibility.

The London Extension

The London Extension began with what at the time appeared to be a relatively innocuous branch from the MS&LR line at Beighton, which lies on the Derbyshire/Yorkshire border, to Annesley in Notts. Here it made an end-on connection with the GNR's Leen Valley line, over which running powers were obtained into Nottingham. The MS&LR branch did include what has been accurately described as a 'grim loop line' from Staveley to Chesterfield and thence on to Heath where it rejoined the Annesley 'branch'. For Watkin the Annesley branch had a dual purpose. One was to gain access via the GNR to the collieries in the Leen Valley. But perhaps more significantly, it would ultimately provide the springboard that would be the beginning of the realisation of his ultimate dream of being the Overlord of a through railway route from the North to the Continent.

At the time, however, Watkin was insistent that Annesley would be the MS&LR's southern outpost. Had his true ambition been known, it is highly unlikely that the GNR would have been so cooperative in respect of running powers. As it was, MS&LR freight trains reached Annesley in October 1892 and passenger trains began working into Nottingham London Road at the beginning of January 1893.

But by then, Watkin had 'nailed his colours to the mast' and declared his intention to build a new independent line from Annesley to London. The first attempt to obtain an Act to build the London Extension was rejected by Parliament in 1892. Watkin was furious, especially as an even more 'pie in the sky' scheme, the Lancashire, Derbyshire & East Coast Railway (see Chapter 7), was approved on the same day. Undeterred, Watkin tried again the following year. This time, no doubt as the result of lobbying his fellow MPs, the application was more successful. A little under three months after MS&LR trains first began to appear in Nottingham, the London Extension Act received the Royal Assent.

But the cost of transforming Watkin's dream into reality would prove to be horrendous. And it wasn't just financial. The social upheaval during construction, particularly in Nottingham, and to a lesser degree in Leicester, was pretty horrendous too.

As we have already seen in the previous two chapters, Annesley, which lies at the head of the Leen Valley, was already served by the both the Midland and the Great Northern. The Midland, whose line through the Leen Valley had opened in 1848, had naturally chosen the easiest route. The GNR line to Annesley through the valley, which had opened in 1881, had been forced to take the second best route. The MS&LR's London Extension had to plot a course through, and make the best of what was left. And with Watkin's eye on potential Continental traffic using the line, he decreed that it would be built to the European 'Berne Gauge', the clearances of which were somewhat more ample than the normal British loading gauge.

That this was achieved, in great style, is indisputable. But it came at a cost. A very high cost. At Bulwell, for instance, a massive 390 yard long, 25 arch viaduct was required. And whereas the Midland's and the Great Northern's lines skirted around the ridge of high ground to the north of Nottingham, the London Extension confronted the problem head-on by boring two separate tunnels under the ridge, the aggregate length of which was over one mile.

The construction of the London Extension was divided into seven contracts. The section between Annesley and East Leake, which was just over 17 miles in length and known as Contract No 1, was awarded to Logan & Hemingway at a cost of £684,451. It was not the lowest tender, but the same firm had acquitted themselves

An 1896 view looking towards the site of the future New Basford station from high above the north portal of Sherwood Rise Tunnel.
(Courtesy of R.H. Bird and Picture the Past)

well during the building of the Beighton to Annesley branch. As probably the No 1 Contract was going to be one of the most difficult, the MS&LR Board obviously adopted the 'better the devil you know' philosophy. The engineer for the contract was Edward Parry whom we met in Chapter 3.

Contract No 2, from East Leake to Aylestone (south of Leicester), was put into the hands of Henry Lovatt & Co of Wolverhampton. Once again, this was just over 17 miles in length. Although Lovatts encountered their own problems in building the line through the centre of Leicester, the first 4 miles or so of their contract, which took the line out of Nottinghamshire into Leicestershire, was a relative cakewalk.

But to return to Contract No 1. After the Bulwell Viaduct, the next major obstacles that Logan & Hemingway had to tackle were the ridges of high ground to the north of the centre of Nottingham. These were penetrated first by the 662 yard long Sherwood Rise Tunnel. After just over 150 yards in daylight, albeit in a 40 feet deep cutting, where the short-lived Carrington station was located, the line plunged into darkness once again through the 1,189 yard long Mansfield Road Tunnel.

The first London bound coal train rumbled along the new line on 26th July 1898. But it was not until 15th March 1899 that passenger services commenced. Such a delay was quite normal to allow all the new embankments, bridges and structures to 'settle' so that any serious problems could be rectified to ensure that passenger services could be operated safely.

That said, when passenger services began, Nottingham's magnificent central station was still 14 months away from completion. In the interim period, the suburban stations at Carrington and Arkwright Street were used.

Nottingham Victoria

As related in Chapter 3, a central railway station was high on the wish list of Nottingham Corporation's Railway Committee. The corporation's own plans drawn up in the early 1880s for such a station were stillborn, so Watkin's plans to take his line through the centre of the town and build a grand central station were enthusiastically embraced by the council.

The 150 yard 'gap' between the south portal of Sherwood Rise Tunnel and the photographer's viewpoint above the north portal of Mansfield Road Tunnel provided the GCR with the site for short-lived Carrington station. Carrington bucked the trend by having two side platforms as opposed to a single island platform, which was the characteristic hallmark of most other London Extension stations. Carrington closed as early as 1928, six months before the 30th anniversary of its opening. In the background, several of the Victorian villas (albeit now rather altered) on Clumber Avenue are nevertheless still recognisable today. The large light rectangle in the centre foreground is the back of the year-stone over the Mansfield Road Tunnel portal. (S.W.A. Newton photograph reproduced by permission of the Record Office for Leicestershire, Leicester and Rutland)

After its initial pique at being hoodwinked by the MS&LR over its future plans, the GNR began to realise that there might, after all, be some advantages in hitching its star to the Watkin bandwagon in Nottingham. The Midland, on the other hand, although invited, had no intention of getting into bed with either the MS&LR or the GNR, or becoming part of a Nottingham Central *ménage à trois*. Its distrust of Watkin was considerable. A similar proposal by the MS&LR for the MR to be a partner in the new Leicester Central station was similarly rebuffed. It has to be said that this was hardly surprising. At Manchester, Sheffield, Nottingham, Loughborough and Leicester, the upstart MS&LR would be in direct competition with the Midland for London traffic. There would be competition for the Midland's local traffic too.

Old loyalties die hard. As related in Chapter 11, some 60 years later, when the nationalised British Railways transferred the London Extension from Eastern Region to the London Midland Region, it was the 'kiss of death'. The closure, rightly or wrongly, of the majority of the route was the inevitable result.

But I digress.

The MS&LR's central station was nominally on a north–south axis, at right angles to the corporation's 1881 proposal. That said, the southern end of the MS&LR station was built on part of the land that had been earmarked for the earlier station. The GNR's 'should we, shouldn't we' dithering about becoming involved with the joint station necessitated the plans to be redrawn to enlarge the buildings and facilities when they did eventually decide to participate. The knock-on effect of this delayed the opening of the station for 14 months after the GCR began passenger services on the London Extension. In the interim period, the suburban stations at Carrington, to the north, and particularly Arkwright Street, to the south, were used for main line services.

Centre stage in this image of a now forgotten age are the two elegant Edwardian ladies with their flowery hats and parasols carefully crossing the tramlines on Milton Street, Nottingham. The backdrop to the scene is local architect Edward Lambert's Neo-Jacobean Victoria station building with its impressive 100 foot high clock tower. The tower, and the Victoria Hotel (just visible on the extreme right) are the only survivors into the 21st century. (Courtesy of Nottingham City Council and Picture the Past)

As related in Chapter 3, clearing the 13 acre site for the new station involved the demolition of 1,300 houses, 24 pubs, a church and the workhouse. Whilst tears were probably shed over the loss of the homes, the pubs and the church, the demolition of the workhouse was

A platform level view of Nottingham Victoria taken soon after opening in 1900 when everywhere was still bright and clean, which I have to say is a far cry from my memories of the station in the late 1950s. The photographer has set up his tripod and camera on Platform 4 (the Down Main) to get this image of a Great Northern 2-4-0 standing on the Up Main (no 7) platform line. The loco has probably worked a stopping passenger train over the ANB&EJR line from Grantham and after stabling the coaches seen in the background on the 'middle siding' the loco is either heading to Colwick for disposal or to be turned on the Victoria turntable ready for the return journey. The clocks on the footbridge, which were installed prior to the decision to name the station 'Victoria', carry the letters 'N J S' – Nottingham Joint Station. (Courtesy of Nottingham City Council and Picture the Past)

no doubt welcomed. But clearing the site was only the overture. The 'first movement' required the excavation of well over half a million cubic yards of mainly sandstone before any platforms could be built and the permanent way laid. The contract for the 'finale', the building of what subsequently became known as Nottingham Victoria station, was awarded to Henry Lovatt & Co who were also the main contractors for the section southward from East Leake. The architect was E.A. Lambert who produced a handsome Neo-Jacobean building fronting Milton Street, the centrepiece of which was a 100 foot high clock tower.

At rail level, Victoria basically consisted of two wide island platforms each just a under a ¼ mile in length. At both ends of each of the island platforms were double track bay platforms, giving a total of 12 platform faces. The majority of northbound

In stark contrast to the apparently clean, smoke-free environment portrayed in the previous illustration, here we see what is probably a Derby to Grantham local re-starting from Victoria's Platform 10, on a miserable, cold, damp winter day. The photographer has superbly captured the atmosphere of the moment, but one has to seriously question the long-term effects of the smoke and grime on the health of those living and working nearby.
(Courtesy of F.W. Stevenson and Picture the Past)

trains used either Platform 1 (slow) or Platform 6 (fast) on the down island platform. Similarly, southbound (up) expresses used Platform 7, whilst most through up local trains were routed through Platform 10. In addition to the two fast and slow platform lines in each direction, goods loops were provided to bypass the outer faces of the platforms.

Controlling movements in, out and through Victoria must have been an absolute nightmare. There was a certain amount of scope for 'playing tunes' using the lines within the station itself, but at the end of the day there was only one northbound entry and exit, and only one southbound entry and exit. Relieving the bottlenecks created by the tunnels that flanked the station was not a wholly insurmountable problem, but neither the GCR, the LNER or BR had either the money or the will to do it.

Having bored and blasted their way from the north through sandstone to reach and create Victoria, the builders were suddenly presented with a somewhat different scenario. The southern exit from Victoria was through Nottingham's commercial centre. To achieve this required another tunnel – the 392 yard long Victoria Street Tunnel. As related in Chapter 3, much of this was constructed by the 'cut and cover' method. Essentially this involves forming a cutting, roofing it over, and then reinstating the ground above to more or less as it was originally. The 'cut and cover' part of Victoria Street Tunnel lay along the line of Thurland Street, on which were located several licensed premises. No doubt most, if not all of these taverns were legitimately frequented by the navvies after a long, hard, 12 hour shift. On the other hand, as we saw in Chapter 3, the proximity of the pubs' cellars to the work site sometimes proved to be irresistible.

After Victoria

The junction where the GCR and the GNR parted company was almost immediately after emerging from Victoria Street Tunnel under Weekday Cross, the GNR heading east towards London Road. The GCR line continued south, high above the streets, homes and commercial properties to the south of the city centre, on what was prosaically known as Viaduct 288. This consisted of a total of 65 blue brick and steel girder spans. The most spectacular of these was the 170 foot long bowstring girder that spanned the Midland station.

Just beyond was Arkwright Street station, which was built on spans number 42 to 52 of the viaduct. This was the main London Extension station until Victoria became fully operational. From then on its importance declined, especially when commuters began deserting the railway for trams, buses and cars. But it was the nearest station to Trent Bridge cricket and football grounds, a fact proudly proclaimed under the station nameboard.

Arkwright Street's other claim to fame was that the 1.45 am express from Marylebone stopped here. This was no ordinary express because the 1.45 am also carried the national newspapers that would be pushed through the letterboxes of thousands of East Midland homes just as dawn was breaking. The 'Newspaper', which only stopped briefly at Rugby and Leicester, was a top-link turn, ranking in importance with the GCR section's two named expresses, *The Master Cutler* and *The South Yorkshireman*. Only a loco in tip-top condition would be rostered to haul the train because of the demanding schedule.

On arrival at Arkwright Street at 4.32 am, hundreds of pre-labelled packs of papers would be unloaded from the train's parcels vans onto platform barrows. These packs were then unloaded from the barrows and 'posted' down spiral, helter-skelter-like chutes to the newsagents' vans waiting in the street below. For 15 minutes the frantic activity on the platform was the scene of organised chaos. Then at 4.47 am, with the papers all unloaded, the guard would give the 'right away' for the train to complete its journey, three minutes later, in Victoria.

Between Arkwright Street and the next major obstacle, crossing the River Trent, the GCR established an extensive goods facility at Queen's Walk. Here in contrast to the geographical and geological restrictions imposed by the Victoria station site, the MS&LR could really spread its wings. The Queen's Walk Goods Depot covered a total of 33 acres and included not only a large bonded warehouse and offices, but a carriage sidings and a loco shed too. Over the years, miles of Nottingham lace, thousands of Raleigh bicycles and millions of John Players cigarettes must have been despatched from Queen's Walk. Add to this similar quantities handled by the Midland's, the Great Northern's and the LNWR's goods depots and the importance of the railways to Nottingham's economy cannot be underestimated.

At the south end of Queen's Walk Yard were a pair of three-span girder bridges that carried the GCR across the Trent. One bridge carried the passenger lines, the other the goods lines. Beyond the Trent the goods and passenger lines combined again.

Compared with the viaducts, cuttings and tunnels that prefaced the arrival and departure of the London Extension through Nottingham itself, the final miles of Logan & Hemingway's Contract No 1, to East Leake, were something of an anticlimax. At East Leake, at the commencement of Contract No 2, Logan & Hemingway handed over to Henry Lovatt & Co of Wolverhampton. The first few miles of the Lovatt contract, which took the line out of Nottinghamshire into Leicestershire, were pretty easy too. A 99 yard long tunnel was necessary to pierce the ridge over which ran the Hathern to Rempstone road and on the outskirts of Loughborough was the eleven-arch blue brick Stanford Viaduct spanning the River Soar to carry the line into Leicestershire.

S.W.A. Newton

No account, however small, of the construction of the MS&LR's London Extension would ever be complete without the inclusion of at least one photograph taken by S.W.A. Newton. This present volume is certainly no exception.

Sidney Walter Alfred Newton was born in Leicester in 1875. His father, Alfred, was the proprietor of a thriving photographic business in the town (it did not become a city until 1919). The wealthier Victorians' fascination for having their likenesses recorded for posterity on photographic emulsions kept Alfred pretty busy, but in addition to his portrait work, he was also commissioned by Leicester Museum to provide it with a photographic record of many of its artefacts. Sidney joined the family business around 1890, whilst still in his teens.

A few years later, in 1894, when work began on the MS&LR London Extension, Sidney Newton was provided with a unique opportunity to record almost every aspect of the construction of the last main line. He grasped the opportunity with both hands. He not only photographed construction works in and around Leicester, he covered the whole route from Annesley to Marylebone.

Looking at the hundreds of images that S.W.A. Newton produced of the London Extension, it would be easy to assume that Sidney was the MS&LR's official photographer. But this was definitely not the case. In reality the record was his own private crusade, financed in part by selling his photographs to the navvies, engineers and other people that he encountered on his many journeys. The fact that he covered the London Extension from end to end is even more amazing because his only means of transport were the existing railways, his bicycle and, as a final resort, his own two feet. Add to that the fact that everywhere he went on his field trips, he would need to carry a rather bulky and heavy, wood and brass half-plate camera, a very sturdy tripod, and goodness knows how many *glass* plates, 6½ inches wide by 4¾ inches high, which would be mounted in heavy lightproof carriers, the magnitude of the task that he accomplished will hopefully become apparent. The weight of his equipment would have been enormous. And riding along unmade country roads and cart tracks in all weathers with his equipment strapped to his bike could not have been an easy matter either.

Yet in spite of Sidney Newton not being the official photographer, he became well known and was welcomed onto all the construction sites. As a thank you, he presented each of the contractors with a leather-bound album of photographs of their section of the contract, together with superlative maps of the contract, which Newton had drawn himself. His draughtsmanship, like his photographic skills, was outstanding. He was an accomplished watercolour artist too.

Sidney remained in the family photographic business in Leicester until the early 1950s when he sold the shop and retired. He died, aged 85, in 1960, but a year or two before his death he offered Leicester Museum his entire collection of around 5,000 glass plates, which at the time were stored in his garden shed. Fortunately, the museum accepted the offer. Had it not, Sidney's absolutely priceless collection would have ended up smashed and lost forever, buried in a landfill site.

Today, the Newton Collection has been split between two keepers. The images directly concerned with the London Extension are in the care of the Record Office for Leicestershire, Leicester and Rutland. The non-railway images, which vividly capture the social life in late Victorian days in the towns and villages near the new line, are housed in English Heritage's National Record Office in Swindon.

It is a fitting tribute to a very remarkable man.

7

Last But Not Least

East and West

The last decade of the 19th century saw the construction of two new lines through Nottinghamshire. One, as we have already seen in the previous chapter, was the Manchester, Sheffield & Lincolnshire Railway's London Extension, whose route through the county was nominally north to south. The second line, which ran at right angles, from west to east, was the Lancashire, Derbyshire & East Coast Railway.

The LD&ECR was the brainchild of William Arkwright, a direct descendent of Sir Richard Arkwright (1733–1792), the inventor and entrepreneur, who was one of the founding fathers of the Industrial Revolution with his cotton mills at Cromford in Derbyshire. In the 1880s William had inherited the family estate at Sutton Scarsdale in Derbyshire, beneath which were considerable coal seams. To exploit the potential mineral wealth on his property to the full, Arkwright planned to bypass what he considered was the inadequate service offered by both the MS&LR and the Midland Railway. His answer was to propose the LD&ECR, which would allow him to develop his collieries and provide him with outlets to the east and to the west. Unofficially Arkwright's eventual railway became known as the 'East and West'.

It was a truly ambitious plan. Starting from new quays built alongside the Manchester Ship Canal at Warrington, the line would have passed through Knutsford and then traversed the Derbyshire Peak District in a series of long tunnels and over unbelievably high viaducts. After the wild Peak District section lay Chesterfield, beyond which was not only Arkwright's estate, but also those of his neighbours, the Dukes of Portland and Newcastle. These two noblemen along with Earl Manners, all having collieries on their estates, were enthusiastic supporters, morally, if perhaps not too financially, of the proposed line.

To the east of the coalfield lay the City of Lincoln, after which the line was to traverse through some relatively easy terrain to Sutton-on-Sea. Sutton was then a small fishing village where the LD&ECR planned to build a deep water harbour from whence coal could be exported across the North Sea to mainland Europe and, hopefully, even beyond.

The main line, from Warrington to Sutton, amounted to some 130 miles. Adding to this just over 40 miles of branch lines resulted in the LD&ECR having the distinction of being the longest railway (in terms of distance) ever to be approved by Parliament in a single Bill.

One of the main objectors to the LD&ECR was the MS&LR. Ironically, on the very same day that the LD&ECR Bill was approved at Westminster, the MS&LR's London Extension Bill was rejected. Perhaps not surprisingly, Sir Edward Watkin, the MS&LR's Chairman, went ballistic, calling the LD&ECR 'one of the maddest schemes to be ever laid before Parliament'.

Although Watkin's London Extension Bill was approved in the following Parliamentary session, his rant about the LD&ECR was, in hindsight, probably justified. The cost of building the whole line was horrendous. It was certainly way beyond the combined finances of Arkwright and his ennobled neighbours.

But enter onto the scene the Great Eastern Railway. With its headquarters at Liverpool Street station in London, its main sphere of influence was in the counties of Essex, Suffolk and Norfolk and on into Cambridgeshire. None of these counties possessed any coal. But the GER, by virtue of its partnership with the Great Northern in a joint line from March in Cambridgeshire, through Lincolnshire and on to Doncaster, had already gained a foothold, albeit a tenuous one, in the Yorkshire coalfield.

With the LD&ECR due to make a connection with the GNR & GER joint line at Pyewipe Junction near Lincoln, the GER could see the potential in supporting the new line. The GER's reward for that support would be access to the north Notts & Derby coalfield. But the support came with strings attached. In return for running powers over the LD&ECR, the GER contributed £¼ million towards the construction of the 38 miles between Chesterfield and the junction with the joint GNR/GER line in turnip fields at Pyewipe. Included, although outside the geographical scope of this narrative, was the LD&ECR's branch from Langwith to Sheffield. But these were to be the limits. The line through the wilds of Derbyshire and beyond through Cheshire to the Mersey had to be abandoned. So too were the lines east of Lincoln and the LD&ECR's grandiose schemes for developing the port facilities at Sutton-on-Sea.

The line opened fully in March 1897. Freight services over the Nottinghamshire section had begun late in 1896 and a limited passenger service between Lincoln and Edwinstowe was inaugurated in December 1896. Edwinstowe was the main station on the Nottinghamshire section of the LD&ECR and the only one in the county where the company provided a refreshment room for the convenience of its passengers.

Whilst essentially a coal carrying railway, the LD&ECR tried to exploit the tourist potential of the line by calling itself the 'Dukeries Route'. This was because of the number of ducal residences (including those of the Dukes of Portland and Newcastle) that lay within easy distance of the line. The list is impressive and includes the estates at Rufford Abbey, Clumber Park and Welbeck. Edwinstowe had the added visitor

The Royal Train hauled by LD&ECR loco no 26, which was the railway's nominated royal train loco, is seen here at Ollerton in September 1906. Having begun life as a purely freight loco, no 26 was plucked from obscurity to become a celebrity because it was deemed that the regular LD&ECR passenger locomotives were too small and not powerful enough to cope with the lengthy and heavy royal trains that were the norm in those days. Rarely, if not uniquely, has a freight engine received such loving care and attention! Many railways used the combination of one, two, three or four lamps carried on the front of the locomotive to identify the train's importance. For instance, a single lamp carried on the bracket below the chimney represented a stopping passenger train. A lamp above each buffer signified an express train. But a train with lamps on all four of the possible positions was VERY special, because it indicated that it was carrying royalty. All four lamps are visible in the photograph. (Courtesy of Nottinghamshire County Council and Picture the Past)

attraction of being near to the 'Major Oak', which is believed to be over 1,000 years old. The hollow trunk of the tree is reputed to have provided a refuge for Robin Hood and his 'merrie men' when hiding from the Sheriff of Nottingham.

Over the years certain railway stations have become well known because of their frequent use by the Royal Family. In the closing years of the 19th and the opening ones of the 20th centuries, Ollerton received a good deal of royal patronage from the heir to the throne, Albert Edward, the Prince of Wales. Later, of course, after the death of his mother, Queen Victoria, in 1901, the Prince at the age of 60 became King Edward VII. It was the St Leger Stakes, which were and still are run every September at Doncaster, that attracted Edward to spend time as a regular autumn guest in one of several stately homes in the Dukeries. Indeed, two of the Prince's own horses, *Persimmon* and *Diamond Jubilee*, won the St Leger in 1896 and 1900 respectively.

Railway enthusiasts will no doubt recognise that the names of both horses were later bestowed by the LNER on their A1/A3 class locomotives. *Persimmon* carried the LNER number 2549 (subsequently 60050 in BR days); *Diamond Jubilee* was respectively 2545 and 60046. Indeed the names of many other St Leger winners were commemorated on the nameplates of the A1/A3 class, all of which were built in Doncaster locomotive works.

To return to matters pertaining to the Lancashire, Derbyshire & East Coast Railway, although the company's head offices were in Chesterfield, its locomotive works was established at Tuxford. But unlike locomotive works such as Derby and Doncaster, which built locomotives, Tuxford was purely a maintenance and repair depot for the locomotives, all of which had been supplied to the company by Kitson's of Leeds. That said, the facilities at Tuxford were comprehensive.

Tuxford was also where the LD&ECR crossed the East Coast Main Line.

A relatively small town (its population today is less than 3,000), Tuxford was once the centre of hop growing in Nottinghamshire, and during the age of steam it could boast having three railway stations. One was on the ECML. One was on the LD&ECR, and the third was at the point where the two lines crossed. This was called Dukeries Junction and it was where it was hoped that thousands of tourists to the Dukeries would detrain from ECML trains and complete their journey on the LD&ECR. Alas, it was not to be.

Passenger revenue on the LD&ECR was never very great, but the freight revenue was. That said, the vast majority of its freight traffic had to be handed on to one of the big companies for delivery to its final destination. Inevitably the LD&ECR became ripe for being taken over by one of its larger neighbours. In the event it was the Great Central (formerly the Manchester, Sheffield & Lincolnshire), which at the time had no actual physical connection with the LD&ECR, that absorbed the little line on 1st January 1907.

Kirkby South Junction was located in a deep cutting, which was originally excavated by the MS&LR as it headed south towards Annesley in 1891. Next on the scene was the GNR whose Leen Valley Extension line, which opened here in 1898, curves off to the right. The final piece in the jigsaw was put in place in 1917 with the opening of the Mansfield Railway, which began just beyond the signalbox. The Mansfield Railway's independent lines ran parallel to the original MS&LR (by now the GCR) lines for several hundred yards in the widened cutting before swinging north. The former GCR/LNER class O4 2-8-0 no 63807 is seen here heading a train of steel bars off the Mansfield branch towards Annesley. The 'kink' at the rear of the train is due to it negotiating the crossover from the branch onto the main line. (Courtesy of Nottinghamshire County Council and Picture the Past)

The Mansfield Railway

In many counties, railway building was all but complete by the close of the 19th century. Nottinghamshire, however, bucked that trend by building several new lines during the 20th century. The first of these was the 11 mile long Mansfield Railway. It began, as had the GNR's Leen Valley Extension line, in the deep and rather remote cutting at Kirkby South Junction, just north of the GCR's Annesley Tunnel. Heading north, stations were provided at Kirkby, Sutton and Mansfield before the line joined the former LD&ECR main line at Clipstone between Warsop and Edwinstowe.

The LD&ECR had originally planned to build a branch more or less along the same route to Mansfield, but the financial restraints imposed on them by the Great Eastern prevented this.

Thus the Mansfield Railway was born out of frustration with the service given by the Midland Railway and the apparent disinterest of both the Great Northern and the Great Central Railways to provide any worthwhile competition. The leading instigator of the campaign was the Bolsover Colliery Company whose mine at Mansfield Crown Farm had begun turning coal in 1905. ('Turn', incidentally, is colliery speak for coal brought to the surface.) The Bolsover Company had been founded in 1889 by Emerson Bainbridge, who was also deeply involved with the LD&ECR. In addition to assisting in the planning of the line, he subsequently became the company's chairman. After sinking two mines in Derbyshire the company spread its wings and moved eastwards into Nottinghamshire. Crown Farm (known locally as 'Crownie') was the first. In the ensuing years it was followed by mines at Rufford (1913), Clipstone (1922) and Thoresby (1928).

Parliament approved the Mansfield Railway Act in July 1910 and the first section from the former LD&ECR (now the GCR) line from Clipstone to 'Crownie' opened just under three years later. In spite of their initial indifference, the potential of the Mansfield Railway seems to have eventually dawned on the Great Central. The prospect of Crown Farm colliery alone turning over a million tons a year jerked the GCR out of its lethargy and although the Mansfield Railway remained wholly independent until the grouping in 1923, it was worked by the GCR from the outset.

Although it was demolished in the early 1970s, this is Mansfield Central Station as viewed from Great Central Road. The tower at the far end of the building housed the goods and parcels lift. (Courtesy of North Notts Newspapers Ltd and Picture the Past)

Passenger services over the Mansfield Railway began in 1917. This must be contrasted with the withdrawal in 1916, initially as a wartime economy, but later to prove permanent, of passenger services on the Nottingham Suburban Railway and the Midland Railway's branch to Watnall and Kimberley.

In Mansfield itself, the company provided a long, but rather narrow four-storey building that must rate pretty highly on the list of the country's more unusual railway stations. The dimensions of the structure were dictated by the fact that the platforms were located atop a high embankment. From street level (Great Central Road) the building's unusual proportions seemed to be even more exaggerated. A nice touch, although one that was never appreciated by the station's passengers, was the stained glass windows on the second floor in what was planned to be the refreshment room. Sadly it never sold a cup of tea or a stale sandwich because it never opened.

Known as Mansfield Central, the 'Central' reflected the involvement of the GCR rather than the station's location in the town. The Midland Railway's station was much more convenient to the town centre. Until closure, most passengers headed south on trains to Nottingham Victoria rather than north to Ollerton. It was a question of 'six-of-one or half-a-dozen of the other'. Trains from the inconvenient Central to Nottingham were generally quicker, and Nottingham Victoria was much handier for the city centre. Trains from the more convenient Midland station in Mansfield generally took longer to reach Nottingham and deposited their passengers somewhat further away from the heart of the city. But even after regular services were withdrawn in 1956, excursions, mainly to the seaside, continued to call at Central for another decade.

It is said that around the platforms there was always a pervading odour of fish because the Mansfield line was the regular route of southbound express fish trains emanating from Grimsby.

The Mid Nottinghamshire Joint Railway

The sinking of the new efficient deep collieries in the heart of Sherwood Forest to the east of Mansfield in the early years of the 20th century was inevitably followed by the construction of railways to serve them. The pits at Rufford, Clipstone and Thoresby have already been mentioned. To this list must be added Welbeck (1915), Blidworth (1926), Ollerton and Bilsthorpe (both 1927). Prior to the grouping in 1923 both the Midland and the Great Central sought to grab a share of the traffic by building competitive lines.

But rather more commonsense prevailed after 1923 when the LMS (who had absorbed the Midland) and the LNER (who had absorbed the GCR) sat down together to plan a 24 mile joint line from Bestwood near Hucknall on the former MR Leen Valley line to Checker House (between Worksop and Retford) on the former GCR main line. The resulting Act for the Mid Nottinghamshire Joint Railway was approved by Parliament in 1926. It was to be purely a freight only line.

Only the seven mile central section from near Farnsfield on the MR's Southwell & Mansfield line to Ollerton on the former LD&ECR was built. It opened in 1931, but the economic depression and the Second World War resulted in neither the northern extension, from Ollerton to Checker House, nor the southern section from Farnsfield to Bestwood being built.

8

The East Coast Main Line

The East Coast Main Line is one of the two main Anglo-Scottish rail arteries linking London (Kings Cross) with Edinburgh. As the name implies, the line runs through the eastern flank of the UK, of which 30 miles (give or take a few yards), from some 3 miles south of Newark to about 8 miles north-west of Retford, lies in Nottinghamshire. But the reference to 'coast' in the title is somewhat misleading. At Newark and at Retford, the North Sea is respectively 37 and 41 miles away as the crow flies. This assumes, of course, that crows actually do fly in straight lines, which seemingly, on long journeys, they do. It is only towards the end of the journey, when the train is north of Newcastle, that the sea is actually near enough to be visible from the train.

Prior to the grouping in 1923, the 393 miles of the ECML were owned by three companies. The southern part, between London and Doncaster (including the section through Nottinghamshire, which opened in 1852) was the Great Northern's. The central section from Doncaster through York and Newcastle to Berwick was North Eastern territory; whilst the remaining 57 mile length north of the border was owned by the North British.

As early as 1860, the three companies had realised the importance of through travel between the two capitals and had got together to finance the building and maintenance of a fleet of carriages, which became known as East Coast Joint Stock. Following the 1923 grouping, all the three companies became part of the LNER group, which simplified the operation considerably.

The *Flying Scotsman* ... I

There can be few Brits who have not heard of the *Flying Scotsman,* which perhaps confusingly, to the uninitiated, is the name of both a locomotive *and* a complete train.

The train came first …

From the early days of the East Coast co-operation, the principal daily Anglo-Scottish express was timed to leave Kings Cross at 10.00 am. The corresponding southbound train was scheduled to depart from Edinburgh's Waverley station at the same time. Soon both trains became known, unofficially, as the *Flying Scotsman* in spite of the fact that in the early days there were regular stops to change locomotives and satisfy the passengers' 'personal needs'. In those early days the overall journey time was 10½ hours. Gradually, thanks to improvements to locomotive performance, this time was progressively reduced. Corresponding improvements were also made to passenger facilities. The latter included the provision of on-train toilets, the introduction of dining cars, carriage warming in the winter and corridor connections between coaches.

The grouping in 1923 brought new challenges. The East Coast lines, which now found themselves all part of the LNER, were still in direct competition with the former West Coast group of companies who had now all become part of the LMS. In spite of various previous east-west agreements on Anglo-Scottish schedules, which in theory were still binding, the stage was being set for some serious rivalry.

Then came the locomotive …

In the last year of its independent existence, the Great Northern Railway built two new large express locomotives with a 4-6-2 (Pacific) wheel arrangement that had been designed by the GNR's Chief Mechanical Engineer, Nigel Gresley. These two locomotives, which were the vanguard of the 'A1' class, incorporated a number of features that, at the time, were towards the cutting edge of technology. That said, they proved to be very successful machines and Doncaster Works had already begun building a further ten of the class when the GNR became part of the LNER on 1st January 1923. The first of the LNER A1s, which was initially given the number 1472, was rolled out of the works in the first month of 1923.

At the time, nobody, but nobody, would ever have dreamed that 1472, later renumbered 4472, would, in time, become not only Britain's most iconic steam locomotive, but arguably, the world's most famous steam locomotive too. Yet even then, the first seeds were already being sown.

One of the first acts of the new publicity-conscious LNER management was to officially bestow the previously unofficial name *Flying Scotsman* on both the 10.00 am from Kings Cross to Edinburgh and the corresponding 10.00 am departure from Edinburgh to London.

The next link in the chain of events was the selection of 4472 to be displayed at the British Empire Exhibition at Wembley in 1924 and 1925, where it was mounted on powered rollers so that the wheels turned slowly and the motion of the valve gear could be clearly seen.

That said, the choice of 4472 for such an auspicious occasion was due to a very inauspicious reason. It had broken down, in service, due to the failure of a key component. The LNER operating department, having been instructed by the top management to supply one of the new A1 class locomotives for the exhibition, decided to 'tart up' 4472, then still awaiting its turn for a major repair at Doncaster, rather than lose one of their operational locomotives for the duration of the exhibition.

For the LNER Publicity Department, the Empire Exhibition proved to be a heaven sent, too-good-to-miss opportunity. So, in spite of the fact that 4472 was what is known in the trade as a 'cripple', it found itself carrying the name *Flying Scotsman* especially for the occasion.

LNER class A1 4-6-2 locomotive no 4472, the Flying Scotsman, *photographed in 1924 after it had been re-railed after its first incarceration at the British Empire Exhibition at Wembley.*
(National Railway Museum/Science and Society Picture Library)

The die had been cast … in more ways than one.

Amongst the many thousands of visitors who admired the magnificent loco at Wembley was an impressionable four year old boy from Nottinghamshire. His name was Alan Pegler. For the youngster, the sight of 4472 at Wembley was a *very* defining moment.

Following a bit of 'tweaking' to another A1 locomotive's valve gear, the coal consumption was reduced by an amazing 20%. This 'tweaking', for the technically minded, was the modification of the piston valve openings from 'short travel' to 'long travel'. It goes without saying that the other A1s were quickly modified accordingly. But in addition to the obvious cost savings, the modified locomotives also made, in theory at least, non-stop running between London and Edinburgh a reality for the first time.

The stumbling block was the problem of crew fatigue, particularly for the fireman. But Gresley (who had subsequently been appointed CME of the LNER) came up with the answer … the corridor tender. In addition to carrying coal and water, Gresley's new tenders incorporated a narrow passageway with a corridor-type connection to the leading coach, which enabled the relief driver and fireman – who up to this point had been travelling in comfort 'on the cushions' in the leading carriage – to swap with the original crew at around the halfway stage of the journey.

Needless to say, it was, in modern parlance, a 'no-brainer' when it came to choosing a locomotive to inaugurate the first northbound non-stop service. So at 10 o'clock on 1st May 1928, 4472 *Flying Scotsman* (now repaired after its incarceration at Wembley) steamed out of Kings Cross. At just after 6 pm she proudly steamed into Edinburgh Waverley.

Her wheels had been turning continuously for exactly 8 hours and 3 minutes.

Amongst those standing on the platform of Barnby Moor & Sutton (the first station north of Retford) to watch 4472 thunder through on the inaugural non-stop run was an eight year old who had first seen the locomotive at the Wembley Exhibition. That boy was Alan Pegler.

Coal and water

The 'tweaking' of the A1 locomotive's valve gear resulted in the average coal consumption being reduced to around 45 lbs per mile.

If 393 miles (the distance between London and Edinburgh) is multiplied by 45 lbs and then divided by 2,240 (so that the answer is in tons), the answer is just under 8 tons. Gresley's corridor tenders held 9 tons of coal, so assuming that the tender was full at the start of the journey, there should have been around a ton of fuel remaining when the train reached its destination. That said, occasionally, after a particularly difficult journey (or indifferent quality coal), it was not unknown to arrive at Waverley or Kings Cross with an empty tender.

On the other hand, running out of water was definitely NOT an option – it was (and still is) a major crime because of potentially very expensive damage that can be caused to the locomotive's firebox. In the event of not being able to get water into the boiler, the standard procedure is to drop the fire and fail the locomotive immediately.

The water consumption of the 'tweaked' Gresley Pacifics averaged out at around 40 gallons per mile. Multiply this by 393 and it can be seen that nearly 16,000 gallons of water were needed be evaporated to get a train from London to Edinburgh. Yet Gresley's biggest tenders only carried 5,000 gallons of water.

With no intermediate stops *en route* where the crew could 'put the bag in' (which is loco speak for topping up the tender from line-side water cranes or water columns), water ***troughs*** were the answer.

There were six sets of water troughs on the ECML, two of which, at Muskham and Scrooby, were in Nottinghamshire. The Muskham troughs had been installed in

1900. The Scrooby troughs followed two years later. For the sake of completeness, the others were at Langley (Hertfordshire), Werrington (near Peterborough), Wiske Moor in North Yorkshire and the final set was at Lucker in Northumberland.

A railway water trough was a continuous shallow metal container, several hundreds of yards in length, approx 18 inches wide by 6 inches deep, laid between the rails. It is perhaps rather stating the obvious, but the essential requirement was that troughs had to be located on perfectly level sections of track.

As the locomotive was passing over a trough, the fireman lowered a scoop, which was located beneath the tender, into the trough. The forward motion of the train provided the momentum to force the water up an inclined pipe above the scoop and into the top of the tender. The length of the trough depended on the location. Both Muskham and Scrooby troughs were around 700 yards in length, which meant that at 60 mph, the fireman had a fraction under 24 seconds in which to lower his scoop, collect as much water as he could, and then raise the scoop again.

Not taking enough water in the available time would doubtless result in the fireman being given a good rollocking by his driver. Taking too much water and overfilling the tender would result in the first coach or two being deluged, and any unsuspecting passenger sitting adjacent to an open window would be treated to a very unexpected cold shower … but with his or her clothes still on! Indeed, the attendants on the ECML Pullman trains, such as the *Yorkshire Pullman* or *The Queen of Scots* had specific instructions to make sure that all the carriage windows were closed as their train approached a set of troughs. However, this was only a precaution as by this stage in their careers the top link East Coast Main Line firemen were, as indeed were virtually all top link firemen, absolute masters of their art.

Trainspotting

From the dawn of the railway age there has always been a band of amateur enthusiasts who have patiently recorded the comings and goings, and the ups and downs of the country's railway systems. Those records of their observations that have survived, especially the early ones, have proved to be a godsend for modern day railway historians. Without them, our knowledge of the activities of the early railway companies, and indeed their successors, would be rather scant.

Inevitably, these enthusiasts began to get together to compare notes and this led to the founding of organisations such as the Stephenson Locomotive Society in 1909. Many others have followed. The Railway Correspondence and Travel Society was formed in 1928. Whilst the title no doubt accurately described the society's activities, it has been irreverently suggested in some quarters that the abbreviated title 'RCTS' actually stands for Royal Corps of Train Spotters!

And talking of trainspotters …

From the earliest days of the railways many small boys collected the numbers (and if applicable, the names) of the locomotives that they saw. It was a completely harmless activity but, at the end of the day, not a very productive one, except perhaps for a collection of notebooks containing the numbers and names of the engines that they had seen. But during the Second World War, all this was to change.

Just before the start of the conflict, a 15 year old by the name of Ian Allan landed a job as a clerk in the Southern Railway's General Manager's office at Waterloo. Amongst the teenager's tasks was responding to enquiries from the public about the Southern Railway's locomotives. In order to do this, he was provided with an official booklet containing the numbers, the names, the type and the shed allocation of every SR locomotive. Presumably to make his own life a little easier, Allan suggested that the booklet be published. The suggestion was initially turned down by the SR management, but he subsequently got permission to publish it, but at his own risk and his own expense.

It was a *very* defining moment …

In 1942 and still only 19 years old, Ian Allan produced the *ABC of Southern Locomotives.* Priced at one shilling each, the initial 2,000 copies were an immediate sell out. Reprints followed, as did subsequent Ian Allan *ABCs* for the other three main line companies' locos. Trainspotting had been born.

But there was a downside.

Some boys became a little too enthusiastic about the new hobby and in 1944 a group of youths were arrested for their own safety after trespassing onto the West Coast Main Line at Tamworth in Staffordshire. The incident made headlines in the national press and, as a result, Ian Allan felt partly responsible. This led him into forming the 'Ian Allan Locospotters Club', which soon had branches up and down the country. The primary objects were to teach railway safety to youngsters and organise official visits to railway works and sheds.

Trainspotting at Newark

It is at this point that I have to declare an interest, not only as a buyer of Ian Allan *ABCs* but as a member of the Locospotters Club. That was in the 1950s, by which time the railways had been nationalised and Ian Allan *ABCs* had been 'regionalised' into Western, Southern, London Midland and Eastern & North Eastern volumes; the locomotives working in the BR Scottish Region appeared in the two latter volumes. By the early 1950s the *ABCs* had increased in price to 2/6d each. A hard-covered combined volume listing all BR locomotives cost 10/6d.

Additionally there was an *ABC Locoshed Book*, which gave the allocation of every BR locomotive. The *ABCs* were published annually, but to keep spotters up to speed Ian Allan had already begun publishing the monthly *Trains Illustrated*, which included details of new locomotives, withdrawn locomotives and changes in shed allocation. For many teenage boys, your author included, the publication of the new season *ABCs* involved many hours of 'transferring' the numbers of the locomotives that they had seen, by underlining each one of the numbers in the new volume.

Being Derbyshire born and bred and travelling to school in Derby by train, I was fortunate to be able to keep a fairly regular eye on the new and overhauled locomotives that were outshopped from the Derby Works. These were almost entirely freight, mixed traffic and secondary passenger locomotives from all over the London Midland region. As is often the case, the grass was much greener on the other side because the glamorous, exciting, express passenger locomotives were overhauled elsewhere: the London Midland's at Crewe, the Eastern Region's at Doncaster.

Both towns were a Mecca for East Midlands' trainspotters. So too were Tamworth and Grantham, but my favourite spot for spotting on the East Coast Main Line was at Newark. I have spent very many happy hours on the platforms of Newark Northgate station with a notebook, my *ABC of Eastern Region Locomotives,* and my 'pack-up' … usually corned beef or spam sandwiches, a few of my mother's inedible rock cakes, a bottle of dandelion and burdock 'pop' and several packets of Smith's crisps. This was in the days before crisps were flavoured. Even salt'n'vinegar and cheese and onion crisps were unheard of, as indeed were ready salted. In those days the salt was supplied in the crisp bag in a little blue waxed paper sachet with a twisted top, so that one could add salt to taste. The downside was finding the 'blue crisp' because inevitably it was always at the opposite end, whichever end of the bag that you had opened! I mention the little blue twist bags because, unknown to me at the time, the majority were produced in the Derbyshire village where I lived. When 'ready salted' became the in-thing and the 'blue crisps' disappeared, many village women found themselves on the dole.

But I have digressed …

Some expresses stopped at Newark, but many did not. The sight and sound of the prime of the Eastern Region's express steam locomotive fleet roaring through the station at 60 or 70 and sometimes 80 or more mph was exciting. Even 50 years and more on, those memories are still exhilarating.

A sequence started when one of the many trainspotters on the platform noticed that one of the semaphore signals on the main line had been cleared for an approaching train, and shouted 'peg on the main'. This would be repeated, almost like a religious chant, down the whole length of the platform until everyone's eyes turned either north or south depending on the direction of the origin of the first shout. Everyone would then watch and wait for the appropriate distant signal to be cleared, which was the indication to the train's driver that the block section ahead was clear. When

A streamlined A4, no 60027, Merlin, *dashes through Newark Northgate in the late 1950s with the up* 'Elizabethan', *a summertime only train that ran non-stop between Edinburgh Waverley to London Kings Cross (and vice-versa). Following the Second World War, the* Flying Scotsman *was timetabled to make some intermediate stops. The non-stop replacement inaugurated in 1949 was initially named* 'The Capitals Limited' *but in Coronation year, 1953, this was changed to* 'The Elizabethan'. (Courtesy of L. Clark and Picture the Past)

it did, the repeated cry went up, 'double', and anticipating that the approaching train would be a non-stop express, everyone retreated to the relative safety of the back of the platform. Eyes and ears then strained for the first hint of the train.

The former LNER and subsequently Eastern Region long haul express locomotive fleet consisted mainly of four classes, A1, A2, A3 and A4. The 'A' signified the wheel arrangement, in this case 4-6-2, otherwise known as a Pacific. The streamlined A4s were the most exciting, especially as one of the class, no 60022, *Mallard*, was, and still is, the holder of the world steam speed record of 126 mph.

In addition to their distinctive art-deco shape, the A4s had a distinctive multi-tone 'chime' whistle. The other ex-LNER Pacifics were fitted with a high-pitched whistle. But given the right wind direction, an A4 could be identified from its whistle long before the train appeared. But whether it was sight or sound, the imminent approach of a streamlined A4 was heralded by a youthful chorus of 'streak'. This was one of many examples of 'spotter speak' that described various classes of locomotive. 'Streak' was pretty obvious but some of the more obscure ones included 'spam can', 'iron lung', 'knick-knack' and 'duck six'. Another commonly used word by trainspotters was 'cop', but this had nothing to do with a member of the local constabulary. As a verb it meant to see a particular locomotive for the first time. The noun meant that particular locomotive at that moment in time.

In the days when I trainspotted at Newark, the most iconic of the streamlined A4s was no 60007, which was named *Sir Nigel Gresley* in honour of the designer of the A4s (and indeed, many other classes of LNER locomotives too). No 60007's status was due to the fact that its regular driver was Bill Hoole of Kings Cross shed whose

A postcard of Newark Great Northern station (later Newark Northgate), looking north, in the early years of the 20th century – some 50 years before I was a trainspotter here. As noted in the main text, a further 50 years on I visited Northgate again and was delighted to see that the wonderful clock, made by Potts & Sons of Leeds in 1883, is still going strong in the 21st century. (Courtesy of the Frank Berridge Collection)

locomotive skills and exploits on the East Coast Main Line had become legendary and were regularly reported in *Trains Illustrated.* On most occasions 60007 would thunder through Newark non-stop, but on the few times that it did stop, it would be immediately surrounded by boys hoping for a glimpse of their hero. Albeit on a somewhat smaller scale, it was the same kind of adulation that the likes of David Beckham receive today.

Just prior to his retirement in 1959, Driver Hoole and 60007 were chosen to work the Stephenson Locomotive Society's 50th anniversary train from Kings Cross to Doncaster and back. For those on board it was a day that they would never forget, culminating in the train attaining the post-war steam speed record of 112 mph during the return journey.

In addition to Driver Hoole, his fireman and a locomotive inspector, on the footplate that day was a 39 year old Nottinghamshire man who had become a successful businessman and had been appointed as a member of the British Transport Commission's Eastern Area Board.

His name, if you haven't guessed it already, was Alan Pegler.

More than 50 years later, whilst writing this book, I revisited Newark Northgate. A lot has changed, but much of the down (northbound) platform seems to have survived, pretty well intact, including the wonderful clock, made way back in 1883 by W. Potts & Sons of Leeds. Clocks tell the time, but what amazing ***stories*** this clock could tell, if only it could speak.

The Newark level crossing

I guess that for most people the term 'level crossing' conjures up an image of a road crossing the railway.

In the age of steam, that image would be of massive, white painted, wooden gates, usually with large round red warning discs mounted on them, being swung across the road by a signalman or crossing keeper to ensure the safe passage of the train. Today, of course, the vast majority of these have been replaced by remotely controlled automatic lifting barriers, which, depending on the location, are either the full or half-barrier variety, or on some minor roads, no barriers at all, just flashing lights.

But on the ECML in Nottinghamshire, at both Newark and Retford, there was another type of level crossing … where one railway crossed another.

At Newark, it was the ECML crossing the Midland Railway's Nottingham to Lincoln line. At Retford, it was the ECML crossing the Manchester, Sheffield & Lincolnshire Railway's main line from Sheffield into Lincolnshire. There were a few examples in other parts of the country, but either through subsequent line closures or the construction of graded crossings – as was done at Retford in 1965 – the last remaining rail-rail level crossing in the country is now just north of Newark.

Former Great Northern Railway class J5 0-6-0 no 65482 trundles a southbound coal train over the Newark level crossing on 23rd May 1953. The MR/LMS line from Newark runs left to right in the foreground and behind the signal cabin towards Lincoln. Behind the rear of the train can be seen the two 'tubular' bridges spanning the Trent Navigation.
(Courtesy of the Frank Berridge Collection)

The MR's Nottingham to Lincoln line (opened in 1846) was the first on the scene in Newark. Indeed it was almost six years later that GNR trains appeared in the town with the opening of the so called 'Towns Line' between Peterborough and Retford in 1852.

It does not take too much imagination to work out the operational, and the potential safety, nightmares that such crossings could cause, particularly when two separate (and competitive) railways were involved. Indeed, until some of the initial problems were resolved, the Midland actually removed the GNR's rails on either side of the crossing to protect their interests. Eventually, a 'truce' was agreed whereby the Midland's trains would take precedence over the GNR's and passenger trains on both lines would take precedence over freight trains on the other's. That said, it did not prevent a GNR passenger train from slicing through a Midland freight train on the crossing a few months later.

The grouping in 1923 did not change matters as the ECML became part of the LNER, with the former Midland line becoming part of the LMS. Indeed, it was not until after nationalisation and some rationalisation of regional boundaries took place in 1950 that the Newark Crossing, as it is now known, became under unified control.

THE *FLYING SCOTSMAN* ... 2

I first saw the *Flying Scotsman* in the late 1950s on one of my trainspotting excursions to Newark. By this time it was carrying its BR number, 60103. Additionally, in 1947, it had received a new higher pressure 220 lbs/sq inch boiler (40 psi more than the original), by virtue of which it was reclassified as an A3.

But back in the 1950s, in an attempt to add a little kudos and stem the rising tide of complaints about the late running and overall poor quality of services on the express services on the former GCR main line out of Marylebone, BR's Eastern Region management decided to transfer *Scotsman* to Leicester. Between June 1950 and November 1953 the *Flying Scotsman*, then renumbered 60103, appeared regularly on express services through Nottingham Victoria.

The age of steam in Nottinghamshire, and in the UK as a whole, was beginning to close when 60103 returned to its original ECML stomping ground in late 1953. The first main line diesels began to appear on the scene in the late 1950s, and the final straw was the introduction of the powerful diesel-electric 'Deltic' locomotives to replace steam on the principal ECML expresses during 1961 and 1962.

The wholesale scrapping of once proud ECML fleet of steamers soon began in earnest.

The *Flying Scotsman*'s last run as a British Railways owned locomotive was from Kings Cross to Doncaster on a snowy 14th January 1963. Crowds, including no doubt many Notts folk, gathered at stations and vantage points along the route to bid farewell to the locomotive, which was celebrating its 40th birthday. But in reality it was to be 'au revoir' rather than 'goodbye' because amongst those on the footplate that day was none other than Alan Pegler, whose offer of £3,000 to buy the loco for preservation had been accepted by BR.

As a member of the BTC Eastern Area Board, Mr Pegler had been in an ideal position to negotiate the purchase of the locomotive that he had first fallen in love with nearly 40 years previously at the Wembley Exhibition. That said, it had NOT been a case of what today could be called 'insider trading'; the negotiations and contracts were all legal and above board ... and completely watertight.

It seems that when news of the deal reached the ears of Doctor Beeching, he went ballistic. But as the agreements were legally binding, there was nothing he could do to prevent the transaction. So instead of joining the long procession of steam locos heading for scrapyards, 60103 returned to Doncaster Works where, as part of the deal, it was overhauled and restored to its LNER condition as no 4472. Once again, nobody, but nobody who was involved at the time would have dreamed of the memorable adventures, and the highs and the lows that were awaiting 4472 in the ensuing years ...

Space precludes telling the full story, but the first really big highlight was the commemoration of the 40th anniversary of her first non-stop London to Edinburgh run on 1st May 1968. At this point in time, the end was rapidly approaching for what remained of BR's steam fleet; the final few would be withdrawn just over three months later. As a consequence of dieselisation, a lot of the former watering facilities along the route had disappeared, so to try to ensure that 4472 would have sufficient water to repeat the non-stop journey, a second tender was acquired and converted into an auxiliary water carrier.

The journey was filmed for posterity by BBC2 and includes some spectacular aerial photography. There were several nail-biting moments when 4472 was slowed to little more than walking pace. But her wheels managed to keep turning and Edinburgh was reached non-stop. Not a bad effort for a 45 year old locomotive with over 2 million miles on the clock.

But as Mr Pegler and the *Flying Scotsman*'s subsequent owners will testify, preserving a steam locomotive and keeping it maintained it to the exacting standards required for main line running is a licence to spend very large sums of money. In an attempt to get *Scotsman* to contribute financially towards its upkeep, Alan Pegler and 4472 set off on a promotional tour of the USA in 1969. Initially, the tour was a success, but things began to go increasingly pear-shaped, culminating in him being bankrupted in 1972.

The immediate future looked bleak for 4472. There was even talk of cutting it up for scrap, but at the eleventh hour a real knight (although not one in shining armour), in the form of Sir William McAlpine, appeared on the scene to rescue the loco. After repatriation to the UK and overhaul, it became a regular performer on main line railtours and made numerous guest appearances on preserved railways up and down the country.

In 1988 the locomotive left our shores again, this time to be part of Australia's bi-centenary celebrations. Whilst down-under and at the ripe old age of 66, *Scotsman* once again broke the world non-stop record for steam. This time, the distance covered was 442 miles.

Now I have to admit that writing about a locomotive's exploits in Australia in the late 1980s seems to be a very long way from the 'Nottinghamshire Railways in the Age of Steam' brief for this book. Yet had it not been for the foresight of Nottinghamshire's Alan Pegler to buy the *Flying Scotsman* from BR in 1963, what is now the world's most famous steam locomotive would, along with every other Gresley A3, be just a fond memory.

As it is, after several more highs and lows, it has rightly become a part of our priceless National Railway Museum collection.

9

Oh, I do like to be beside the seaside...

Today, loyalty to one's employer, particularly in some of the financial business sectors, seems to be a fast disappearing, if not a totally forgotten, trait. Yet during the golden years of steam, for many, whatever their occupation, loyalty was the norm.

Sons followed their fathers into the same factory, or down the same mine, just as their fathers had followed their fathers. On the female side, there were instances of daughters following in their mothers' and grandmothers' footsteps too. In many workplaces in the industrial East Midlands, and elsewhere in the country, it was certainly not uncommon to find several branches, and several generations of the same family, both male and female, employed by the same firm.

As a way of saying 'thank you' to their workforce for this loyalty, some of the more enlightened employers organised a free, or at the very least, a heavily subsidised annual outing. The destination of many of these trips was often the seaside.

One of the earliest pioneers of employee welfare was Boots the Chemists. John Boot had opened his first shop selling herbal remedies in Nottingham in 1849, but it was his son Jesse who became the driving force behind the development of the business. His philosophy was 'philanthropic retailing' – selling medicines at prices that even the poor could afford. It was, as history has proved, a winning formula. But Jesse Boot was conscious that a lot of the credit for his success was due to the loyalty of his employees.

As early as 1887 Boots had began to organise outings for their employees. The destinations of the first few seem to be lost in the mists of time, but in 1892 the Midland Railway provided a train for the 11 mile journey to Bleasby on the Lincoln line. Here 'the chemists, clerks and draymen, artists, printers, joiners, painters, plumbers and polishers' alighted to walk to Hazelford Ferry, 'a lovely spot on the

A postcard of Bleasby station taken some 20 years after it was the destination of the 1892 Boots outing. The reverse of the postcard, which was written at the Manor House at Bleasby on 4th June 1913, makes interesting reading. 'This is our station. The 4.30 milk train is just coming in. Everywhere is looking lovely. We went over the Trent on Sunday Evening. Can get a glorious view for miles around.' (Postcard courtesy of the Frank Berridge Collection)

banks of the Trent. A substantial dinner was served at the Star and Garter followed by sports in the afternoon and dancing in the evening.'

The destination for the 1894 staff outing on August Bank Holiday Monday was a visit to the caverns at Castleton in the Derbyshire Peak District followed by an open air picnic. Once again, the Midland Railway provided the train, the final few miles being over the Midland's brand new Hope Valley line that had then only been open for two months. For the event the company produced a special 24 page souvenir booklet, which was 'Printed at Boots Steam Printing Department' and described the route that the train would take and also the attractions of Castleton. To ensure that the event was recorded for posterity, Jesse Boot and his wife Florence arranged for the picnic to be photographed. Everyone present received a print. For many, it would have been the first and probably the only time that they ever appeared on film.

The East Midland's towns and cities, including Nottingham, are amongst the furthest away from any part of the English coast. Yet displayed on the notice boards on every

One of the many versions of the Jolly Fisherman – Skegness is SO Bracing – posters, originally commissioned by the Great Northern Railway in 1908. (Author's Collection)

railway station, large or small, were gaily coloured posters extolling the virtues of various seaside resorts. The most iconic of these has to be John Hassall's 'Jolly Fisherman' poster advertising the bracing air of Skegness. This delightful piece of artwork celebrated its centenary in 2008. 'Jolly' can legitimately claim to be one of the world's most iconic posters, but the artist only received a meagre 12 guineas for it. In some ways this was the portent of things to come because in spite of his undoubted talent Hassall was penniless when he died in 1948. His original artwork was presented by British Railways to Skegness in 1966 and it now takes pride of place in the resort's Town Hall.

Yet for many Nottinghamshire folk, these images were just a dream. Skegness (or 'Skeggy' as it is known locally), which was one of the nearest seaside resorts, could well have been on the other side of the world. But for those who were fortunate enough to work for one of the more socially aware employers, a few hours strolling along the Prom (prom, prom) whilst the brass band played 'tiddley-om-pom-pom' even for just a few hours, once a year, was something to look forward to and savour.

By 1902, Boots had abandoned picnicking in Derbyshire and selected 'Skeggy' as the venue for the outing for the lady clerks and the warehouse staff. A copy of the programme of the day's activities, which has survived and is now in the Boots archive, is an absolute gem, as you can see. Interestingly, the outing commenced at London Road Low Level station, which was then a shadow of its former self after most services had transferred to Victoria in May 1900.

The 1908 outings also used the Low Level station. This time the destination was the Franco-British Exposition at the White City in London but on this occasion there was a strict segregation of the sexes. The female staff outing was first on 25th July. The male employees had to wait until 15th August for their turn.

Probably Boots' biggest outing was the one in 1924 when the company took 5,500 of its employees to the British Empire Exhibition at Wembley. On paper, the exercise

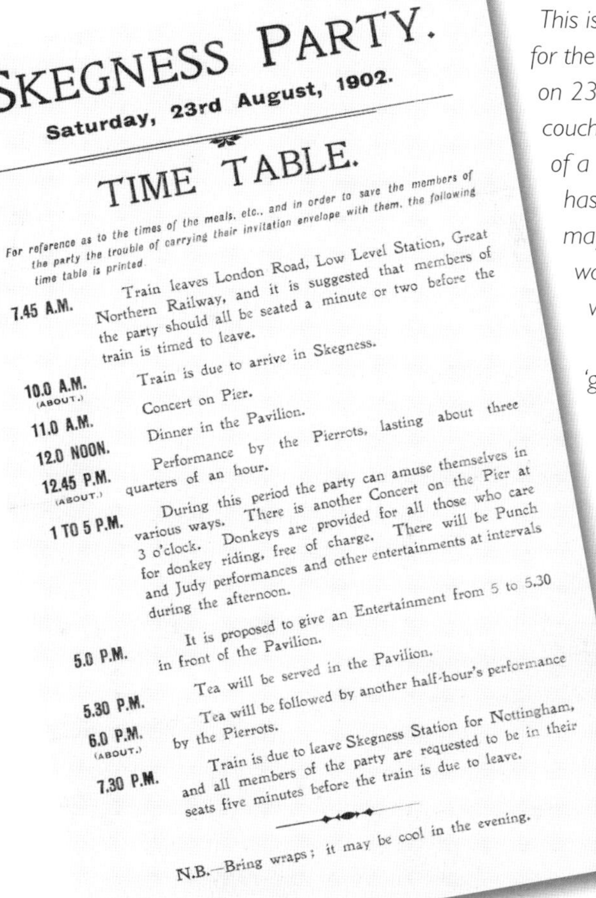

SKEGNESS PARTY.

Saturday, 23rd August, 1902.

TIME TABLE.

For reference as to the times of the meals, etc., and in order to save the members of the party the trouble of carrying their invitation envelope with them, the following time table is printed.

7.45 A.M.	Train leaves London Road, Low Level Station, Great Northern Railway, and it is suggested that members of the party should all be seated a minute or two before the train is timed to leave.
10.0 A.M. (ABOUT.)	Train is due to arrive in Skegness.
11.0 A.M.	Concert on Pier.
12.0 NOON.	Dinner in the Pavilion.
12.45 P.M. (ABOUT.)	Performance by the Pierrots, lasting about three quarters of an hour.
1 TO 5 P.M.	During this period the party can amuse themselves in various ways. There is another Concert on the Pier at 3 o'clock. Donkeys are provided for all those who care for donkey riding, free of charge. There will be Punch and Judy performances and other entertainments at intervals during the afternoon.
5.0 P.M.	It is proposed to give an Entertainment from 5 to 5.30 in front of the Pavilion.
5.30 P.M.	Tea will be served in the Pavilion.
6.0 P.M. (ABOUT.)	Tea will be followed by another half-hour's performance by the Pierrots.
7.30 P.M.	Train is due to leave Skegness Station for Nottingham, and all members of the party are requested to be in their seats five minutes before the train is due to leave.

N.B.—Bring wraps; it may be cool in the evening.

This is the timetable for the outing to Skegness for the Boots lady clerks and the warehouse staff on 23rd August 1902. Its appeal is because it is couched in such genteel language – almost that of a forgotten age. But, the pièce de résistance has to be the final footnote to 'Bring wraps; it may be cool in the evening.' I suspect that this was probably instigated by Mrs Boot herself, who took a very keen maternal interest in the health and welfare of her husband's 'girls'. (Image by courtesy of the Boots UK Archive)

could have resulted in a logistical nightmare, both for the company, and for the LNER, but thanks to excellent planning on both sides, the day was nothing less than an outstanding success.

It required no fewer than eight special trains to carry all the passengers. This time the starting point was Nottingham Victoria because the route to Wembley Hill was over the former GCR London Extension. The first train pulled out of the station at 5.47 am; the eighth, and last, at 9.05 am. In between, and all along the route, paths had to be found to accommodate the Boots Specials without delaying scheduled services, be they express, slow passenger or freight trains.

On arrival at Victoria the staff were greeted by a large banner, which was hung from the roof over the entrance proclaiming that the 'Boots Wembley Specials start from Platforms 7 and 10' (these were the main southbound departure platforms). That was just the beginning. Each of the specially polished locomotives carried a large circular headboard on its smokebox, informing the world that the train was the 'Boots Wembley Express' together with a letter identifying the train. And to try to ensure that nobody got on the wrong train, stickers such as 'Boots for Wembley – F' had been placed in every carriage window.

Having arrived at Wembley there were a bewildering number of exhibition pavilions to visit. Most were dedicated to specific countries that were part of the then still great British Empire. In these were exhibited the native arts, crafts and cultures of that country. But there were other attractions. No doubt, for the men at least, these included The Palace of Industry where amongst the items on display was the LNER's *Flying Scotsman* locomotive (see Chapter 8). But high on the list of priorities for most, if not all, of the Boots staff after detraining at Wembley was a visit to the re-creation of the long lost medieval London Bridge, on which originally there were shops. One of the numerous 'quaint little shops' re-created especially for the exhibition just happened to be a branch of Boots the Chemists. Another feature of the exhibition was a large fun-fair with a selection of what were then state of the art 'white knuckle' rides. Doubtless at least some of these would have been sampled before the exhausted revellers boarded the trains back to Nottingham.

A group of cloche hatted Boots ladies posing by the open windows of one of the special trains to the British Empire Exhibition at Wembley on 21st June 1924. The style of the ribbons decorating this type of hat often signified that the wearer was either married, engaged or 'single and available'. (Photograph by courtesy of the Boots UK Archive)

It did not take long for some of Nottingham's other major employers to follow the Boots lead, amongst them being the Home Brewery and the Daybrook Laundry. I have no doubt at all that the brewery's outings were somewhat less 'structured' than the Boots outings and that the resort's pubs did a roaring trade during the day!

The Home Brewery had been founded at Daybrook (on the outskirts of Nottingham) back in 1875 on the site of a natural spring, by two brothers, John and Samuel Robinson, who named the company after their family home, the Home Farm. Not content with just having the brewery, the Robinson brothers went on to establish the Daybrook Laundry, also on the site of another natural spring but on the opposite side of the road to the brewery. John ran the brewery; Samuel the laundry. Over the years, both the brewery and the laundry went from strength to strength and became household names locally.

The brewery, which was known as 'Home Ales', eventually had a portfolio of over 500 tied pubs. Latterly it was the sponsor of both Notts County FC and the Nottingham Playhouse. Its trademark was (perhaps inevitably) a silhouette of Robin

There is no real need to record that this was taken on the occasion of the Home Brewery trip to Skegness in 1927 as the photographer has already done the job. What isn't stated is that the location is Daybrook station on the GNR's 'Back Line' and it appears to be a specially posed shot with the loco stopped halfway along the platform. Note that virtually everyone, male and female, is wearing a hat. Doubtless the throngs on the platform are concealing numerous crates of the brewery's own bottled products for consumption to help to pass the time away during the 80 mile journey each way. (Courtesy of Nottinghamshire County Council and Picture the Past)

Hood firing an arrow. Eventually it was gobbled up by the Scottish & Newcastle group in 1986. Inevitably, from there on, the road was downhill until the eventual closure of the brewery ten years later.

The Daybrook Laundry fared only a little better.

By 1910 the company was employing over 600 people (mainly female) who washed, dried and ironed around 100,000 items per week for 4,000 customers. This was in the days before hydro extractors (the name given to professional mega-size spin dryers) and tumble dryers. Behind the laundry were 'drying fields' where the washed items were pegged out on lines to dry. This was not a problem on nice warm sunny summer days. But in the winter and during prolonged periods of rain, the backlog of laundry waiting to be dried just does not bear thinking about. With the

From almost the same viewpoint as the previous photograph, but six years on, the Daybrook Laundry girls pose before their trip to Skegness in 1933. Notice that the women wearing hats are now very much in the minority. Note too that the females outnumber the males by a ratio of at least 50 to 1. Perhaps of more interest to railway enthusiasts is that the two coaches visible in the picture suggest that the LNER has rostered one of its new 12-coach green and cream liveried 'tourist' sets for the trip. Most LNER coaches of the period were varnished teak. The building of 10 of these 'tourist' trains in 1933 to replace the rakes of ancient and often rather decrepit coaches that were traditionally used on excursion trains was an attempt to counter the ever growing threat from charabancs. (Courtesy of Nottinghamshire County Council and Picture the Past)

advent of domestic washing machines in the 1950s, the company moved towards the commercial market laundering linen for restaurants and hotels. That too proved to be a dwindling market and following a take-over in 2002, after 127 years of serving the community, the laundry closed.

As noted in the earlier chapters, coal mining has provided a major contribution to Nottinghamshire's history. That said, with a few exceptions, many mine owners, large and small, cared little for the welfare of their employees. This ultimately was one of the several factors that led to the General Strike of 1926.

In an attempt to combat this, many coal mining communities established Miners' Welfare Clubs where the colliers and their families could relax and socialise. These were normally financed and run by the miners themselves. As well as having the inevitable bar (where the beer was usually several pence cheaper than in the local pubs), most miners' welfares had a reading room, snooker and billiard tables and a large hall for meetings, dances and other entertainment. Many 'welfares' had their own football and cricket teams. Indeed, both the cricketers Harold Larwood and Bill Voce, whose bodyline style of bowling terrified the Aussies and decisively won The Ashes for England in the 1932/3 Test series, had worked in Nottinghamshire collieries. Doubtless, both had begun their careers playing for Miners' Welfare cricket teams.

As elsewhere, the highlight of the year for the residents of many mining communities was a day at the seaside, organised, of course, by the miners' welfare. Often it required more than one train to carry all the passengers. In such cases, the first train departed at the 'crack of dawn' – a 5 am start was not unusual. One such outing in July 1929 from Firbeck Colliery at Langold in the north of the county was recorded for posterity in photographs now in the care of the Picture the Past collection.

Firbeck Colliery, which was sunk in 1923, was served by a branch from the South Yorkshire Joint Railway. In contrast to the usual hostility and cut-throat competition

A group of Firbeck Colliery miners and their families pose for the camera before boarding the train for the annual outing in July 1929. The destination on this occasion was Blackpool. The location is the colliery sidings. Hopefully, the early morning mist apparent in the photograph will soon lift and it will be a nice bright sunshiny day. Note that as with the Home Brewery outing, most of the trippers seem to be dressed in their 'Sunday best', including, of course, a cap or hat. Note too that the newspaper sellers seem to be doing a good trade.

(Courtesy of Nottinghamshire County Council and Picture the Past)

Another wonderfully evocative record of the Firbeck Colliery outing to Blackpool. This time an enterprising local trader has set up a stall selling 'must-have' accessories for a trip to the seaside, including buckets and spades, cricket bats, parasols, flags and windmills.
(Courtesy of Nottinghamshire County Council and Picture the Past)

between the larger pre-grouping railways, the South Yorkshire Joint, whose origins date back to 1903, was a true 'joint' line. It was the result of co-operation by five companies: the Great Northern, Great Central, Great Eastern, the Lancashire & Yorkshire and the Midland. Each had a 20% share in the SYJR, but following the 1923 grouping the LNER became 60% owners with the LMS having the remaining 40%. This is reflected in the illustrations. The coaches in the first photograph are LMS period 1, two-window vehicles, whilst the locomotive visible in the second illustration appears to be an LNER 'J6' locomotive.

The 'sting-in-the-tail' for the Firbeck day trippers was the fact that although the colliery was only 4½ miles as the crow flies from Worksop, it is 17½ miles by rail. Quite a large proportion of this was over lines that normally only carried coal trains. Special permission to run passenger trains on freight lines was (and still is) necessary and if that authorisation is given, numerous additional safety requirements and severe speed restrictions are usually imposed. Local legend has it that the speed limit for passenger trains on the Firbeck branch was only 5 mph, so in effect, it took longer to get to the main line at Worksop than it did for the rest of the 100 mile journey from Worksop to Blackpool.

On the return journey it is said that many of the trippers jumped off the train at Worksop and ***walked*** back home because it was quicker!

10

New King Coal

As we have seen in earlier chapters, Nottinghamshire's first railways – the Wollaton Rayleway of 1604 and the Mansfield & Pinxton Railway of 1819 – were both built to support their local coal mines. Equally, the original aim of the Midland Counties Railway, as proposed in 1832, was to carry Erewash coal to Leicester. Admittedly, that scheme was temporarily hi-jacked in favour of passenger lines. But eventually, when the Midland Railway built and opened the line along the Erewash Valley to serve the existing collieries, it was the catalyst for new mines to be sunk.

It was the start of an oft repeated scenario. When new lines opened, such as the Midland Railway's line through the Leen Valley towards Mansfield, the landowners alongside the route could see the potential in exploiting the mineral resources under their estates. The MR line through the Leen Valley triggered a rush to open new mines. Two were sunk at Hucknall in 1861/1862. These were followed at intervals until 1875 by others at Annesley, Bestwood, Linby, Newstead and Radford.

In the beginning, the Midland Railway held an almost complete monopoly of moving Nottinghamshire coal. But the Great Northern, eager to get a slice of this rich cake for itself, began to break the monopoly, first with its line along the Erewash Valley to Pinxton in 1875, and then through the Leen Valley to Annesley in 1882. It has to be said that the colliery owners were delighted by the arrival of the GNR. It enabled them to play one railway against the other in order to obtain the most competitive transport rates. And where the 'main line' companies feared to tread, the colliery owners did the job themselves and built their own lines. As related in Chapter 2, Barber, Walker & Co had its own private railway system connecting its collieries. But at both ends of its lines, at Watnall and near Eastwood, connections were made to both the MR and GNR.

Another example was the private railway network created by the Babington Coal Company's owner Thomas North, which totalled around 28 miles in length. Centred on Cinderhill Colliery (now the site of the Phoenix Park terminus of the Nottingham trams), it connected with both the MR and GNR near Bulwell. One of the lines headed towards Nottingham itself, whilst the other headed in the opposite direction linking the Babington Co's other pits before making a connection with the MR at Ilkeston Junction in the Erewash Valley.

It goes without saying that moving coal from the colliery to its destination required wagons. The mine owners had two choices. They could either utilise wagons hired from the 'main line' companies, or use their own vehicles (either bought outright or leased). Provided that these conformed to the rigid dimensional and quality standards laid down by the Railway Clearing House (RCH), they could be used on the main line railways.

Using railway owned wagons could often result in something called 'demurrage', which in today's parlance is equivalent to a parking fine. There was a 'free period' – usually 24 or 48 hours – during which time the wagon had to be loaded or unloaded. But if this had not been done, then the 'demurrage' charge kicked in. Many collieries preferred to use their own wagons, which, when new, were painted in all the colours of the rainbow. However, after a few trips from the mine to the customer and back, the shiny surface became coated with coal dust, soot and grime and tended to look like almost any other railway wagon.

One trick used by the Midland Railway was to use a special white paint to emblazon the letters 'M' and 'R' on the side of their wagons. This paint contained a special ingredient – oxalic acid, which occurs naturally in spinach and rhubarb. Commercially, the acid has a bewildering variety of uses from de-rusting metal components and polishing marble, to sterilising beer lines in pubs and keeping honey bees free from mites. Additionally, when mixed in the correct proportions with paint, this versatile compound gives the surface self-cleaning properties. So no matter how much filth got plastered on the sides of their wagons, the Midland's 'M R' remained clean and bright.

The demand for wagons spawned a number of specialist businesses who supplied not only private companies, but also on occasions the main line companies too. One, happily still in business at the time of writing and celebrating its centenary in 2010, is W.H. Davis Ltd of Langwith whose works lie on the Notts/Derbys border. Its products today are rather more sophisticated and much higher tech than the thousands of seven-plank, wooden bodied coal wagons that the firm formerly produced.

Another such company was William Rigley & Sons Ltd, whose works at Leen Valley Junction and Bulwell Forest were located alongside the GNR's Leen Valley line. Founded in 1890, it too built thousands of wooden bodied wagons to satisfy the voracious appetite for such vehicles. But times changed and sadly Rigley's seem to have failed to respond to that change. By the 1960s the company's main activity was cutting up for scrap many of the steam locomotives that had regularly hauled Rigley-built coal wagons from the pits to the customer, returning with the empties.

The handling of these wagons was a logistical nightmare. Every wagon, whether

Mansfield Crown Farm Colliery, photographed in the early years of the last century with a brace of Midland Railway 0-6-0s centre stage; Johnson-designed no 3383 is piloting Deeley no 3588. On the left are two wagons owned by Bolsover Colliery Co who had begun turning coal at Crown in 1906. On the right hand side of the lines is a stockpile of pit props.
(Courtesy of the Frank Berridge Collection)

railway owned or privately owned, carried a stiff card label secured in what looked like a large mousetrap on each side of the solebar (the chassis). This label indicated the starting point of the wagon's journey and its destination. But of course, not every wagon from each colliery was bound for the same destination. In order to try to bring some kind of order out of this potential chaos, the principal players built huge marshalling yards where the wagons could be sorted.

The Midland's answer was to build a massive marshalling yard at Toton near Long Eaton. The Great Northern chose Colwick, just to the east of Nottingham for its major sorting sidings. The MS&LR/GCR selected Annesley, at the head of the Leen Valley as the site for its main yard in the county. But it was two-way traffic. Returning empty privately owned wagons to the correct colliery was equally as complicated.

In simple terms, Annesley, Colwick and Toton consisted of one or more 'down' yards and one or more 'up' yards. The 'down' yards handled wagons (mostly empties) heading north; the 'up' yard dealt with wagons (mostly loaded) heading for the south. Annesley, which was the smallest of the three, had a capacity of over 1,100 wagons in its down yard and almost 1,700 wagons in its up yard. The situation at Colwick was somewhat more complicated because separate yards were provided for the use of the LNWR.

The Annesley Dido

Compared to the marshalling yards and loco sheds at Colwick and Toton, which were both located quite close to populated areas, the GCR's yard and loco shed at Annesley were rather 'out in the sticks'. Consequently, many of the staff had to commute the half-a-dozen or so miles from Hucknall or Bulwell, on their own special train known as the 'Annesley Dido'. Essentially, the Dido was similar to the miners' Paddy trains described in Chapter 5 as it consisted of a set of well superannuated coaches. These, it seems, were rarely cleaned, resulting in the floor being 'carpeted' with empty cigarette packets, struck matches and fag ends. Some of the trains used the former GNR Leen Valley line, whilst others were routed along the GCR main line.

The origin of the name 'Dido' has been lost in the mists of time, but a commonly held theory is that as it ran 365 days a year, it is an abbreviation for **D**ay-**I**n, **D**ay-**O**ut.

The last Dido ran in September 1962 ... and was replaced by a bus.

Toton Yard

Some idea of the complexities of a marshalling yard can be gleaned from the aerial picture opposite. The through Erewash Valley passenger and freight lines are the 'straight as an arrow' tracks running almost vertically through the centre of the photograph. To the left of these are the down yards, known as 'The North Yard' (nearest the main line) and the 'Meadow Yard'; it is difficult to tell from the viewpoint of this picture where North finished and Meadow started. Each of the total of 35 lines in the two yards were reserved for wagons for a specific destination. The smoke and steam drifting east from the far end of the down yard are from Toton shed. In addition to stabling and servicing the shunting locomotives that worked in the yard, over 100 freight locos were allocated to the shed for working the trains in and out of the yard. Occupying most of the photograph to the right of the through lines is the West Yard, to the right of which again is the East Yard. Once again, each of the 37 roads was allocated to a specific destination.

Many of the southbound coal trains leaving Toton were heading for the marshalling yard at Brent, near Cricklewood, a few miles to the north of London. From here, wagons would be distributed to coal merchants throughout the Metropolis and the Home Counties. Because of quite severe weight restrictions on many of the bridges on the Midland line to London, the use of big heavy locomotives to haul the Brent bound trains was not an option. As a result many of the coal trains needed to be double-headed. The plus side of this was that by double heading, the number of trains heading south was effectively halved, giving a better line occupation. The minus side was the cost of using two locomotives, two drivers and two firemen.

After the grouping in 1923, in an attempt to reduce costs on the Toton to Brent operation, the LMS ordered a number of articulated Garratt-type locomotives from Beyer, Peacock & Co. Essentially, a Garratt locomotive had two independent, opposite facing, sets of wheels and cylinders. Over one set of wheels was mounted a large water tank; the other set of wheels carried the coal bunker. Between the two, with pivots at either end, were the boiler and the cab. Although somewhat unconventional looking, over 1,600 Garratts were built and worked successfully in Africa, Asia, Europe, South America and Australasia.

A total of 33 Garratt locomotives were delivered to the LMS between 1927 and 1930. The LMS specified that the locomotives should incorporate a number of its own standard components. This was laudable in theory, but in practice the specified components were somewhat inferior to those that would normally be used by Beyer. The ironic result was that the LMS Garratts were probably the least reliable of the

A 1930s aerial view looking north over a part of Toton Yard, taken after a snowfall. The snow would have been a headache for those on the ground, both in terms of keeping the points clear and the potential danger to human life and limb through slipping. On the other hand, from the air, the snow has accentuated the delicate tracery of the miles of trackwork and has produced a fascinating, almost surreal, view of the yard. (Courtesy of Mrs P.A. Brown and Picture the Past)

Bathed in evening sunshine, former LMS Beyer-Garratt 2-6-0+0-6-2 carrying its BR number 47967 clatters past Stapleford & Sandiacre station into the north end of Toton up yard in the mid 1950s. They were impressive locos. They were 87' 10½" in length and weighed 155½ tons. But when this load was spread over 8 axles it was not a problem when crossing the weak bridges on the Midland main line. Stapleford & Sandiacre station, which was a victim of the Beeching axe, closed, along with the other remaining Erewash Valley line stations, on 2nd January 1967. A few traces of the station still remain, as do the shops to the right of the Palace Cinema. The cinema, now long demolished, is like the LMS Garratts … just a memory. (D.B. Swale photograph in the Author's Collection)

genre when compared with the Garratts working elsewhere in the world.

Over half the class were allocated to Toton; the remainder were shared between Hasland (Chesterfield) and Wellingborough. For over a quarter of a century these huge machines were a familiar sight on the Midland main lines in Nottinghamshire and beyond *en route* to London and Birmingham.

Calverton, Cotgrave and Bevercotes Colliery Lines

As noted in several previous chapters, continuing improvements in mining technology enabled deeper shafts to be sunk so that the deep coal seams in the concealed coalfield could be exploited. This was particularly evident in the decade following the First World War, which saw new mines opening at Clipstone (1922), Firbeck and Harworth (both 1923), Blidworth (1926) and Ollerton (1927). The following year, production started at Bilsthorpe and Thoresby Collieries. Inevitably all were connected to one or more of the main line railways.

However, Nottinghamshire's last three new mines, at Calverton, Cotgrave and Bevercotes, all required the building of expensive branches to connect them with the main railway network.

Work on the Calverton site started in 1937. Progress was quite leisurely and it was not until May 1939 that the sinking of the first shaft was completed. The outbreak of the Second World War brought progress almost to a halt and it was 1947 before the sinking of a second shaft began in earnest. In anticipation of the colliery opening and with promises of it yielding a million tons a year for 125 years, the LMS and LNER sought, and obtained, parliamentary powers to build a joint 7-mile double track branch, with connections from both their Leen Valley lines at Bestwood to the colliery. The branch and the colliery (both by then in public ownership) opened in 1952. As such, the branch was the first new line to be opened by BR.

The 125-year life was a pipe dream. The colliery closed in 1999, after just 47 years.

Next in the frame was the Cotgrave Colliery. The main shafts were sunk between 1956 and 1960 and the colliery began turning coal in 1964. With the proliferation of coal fired power stations in the Trent Valley in the 1950s and 1960s (see below) that were either on-line or under construction, the prospects for Cotgrave seemed bright. To cope with the anticipated traffic, BR built a brand new 1¾ mile long branch from the south side of the original GNR (ANB&EJR) bridge spanning the Trent at Colwick. It was an expensive exercise, as a new reinforced concrete viaduct was necessary across the Trent's floodplain.

The geological assessment of the colliery's potential proved to be seriously flawed, particularly in respect of the quality of the coal. It closed in April 1993. After the Colwick yards closed in 1970, Toton became responsible for handling the rail-borne output from the mine.

The third and final post-war pit to be opened in Nottinghamshire was at Bevercotes. Being the most easterly of the collieries in the 'concealed coalfield', its shafts were over ½ mile deep. Once again BR had to construct a new line to serve the mine. This time it was a 4¼ mile branch from the former LD&ECR line. Just as the Cotgrave branch had required some serious engineering with the viaduct over the Trent floodplain, the branch to the new Bevercotes branch necessitated the boring of a 350 yard long tunnel beneath Boughton Brake.

The Trent Valley power stations

When the newly nationalised British Electricity Authority (the forerunner of the Central Electricity Generating Board) began looking for new power station sites in the 1950s, the Trent Valley became a prime choice. Not only would the river and its many tributaries provide all the necessary cooling water for the stations, the proximity of fuel was a key factor. With coalfields in Staffordshire, Warwickshire, South Derbyshire, the Erewash Valley and in Nottinghamshire itself, the Trent Valley was ripe for plucking.

Thus it was that in the 1950s and 60s and even into the 70s a string of coal-fired power stations sprang up alongside the Trent. The first, in terms of it being the nearest to the river's source, was at Rugeley in Staffordshire. The first station on the site was decommissioned in 1995, but the adjacent Rugeley 'B' still feeds up to 1,000 megawatts into the National Grid. Still in Staffordshire, but now just a memory, were the three power stations at Drakelow, just south of Burton-on-Trent. At their peak the three stations together could generate over 2,100 MW, making it, during one period, the largest power station in Europe.

Moving on into Derbyshire, the five cooling towers of the two Willington power stations remain, some 15 years after the rest of the station was closed and demolished. Further down the Trent and on into Leicestershire was Castle Donington power station, which was in operation between 1958 and 1994.

Continuing into Nottinghamshire, and still generating, is the huge Ratcliffe-on-Soar power station whose output of 2,000 MW is sufficient to cater for the needs of 2 million people. To try to put this into some sort of context, the total population of Nottinghamshire at the last count was just over ¾ million.

In Nottingham itself was the small, older and originally municipal owned North Wilford Power Station, which was pretty much self sufficient for coal as it was literally next door to Clifton Colliery. Compared to its Trentside neighbours it was rather small fry and closed when the new larger, more efficient stations came on stream.

Near Newark, a brand new, fuel efficient and environmentally friendly combined cycle gas turbine (CCGT) station is being built on the site of the earlier Staythorpe 'A' (1950–1983) and Staythope 'B' (1962–1994) coal fired plants. The new Staythorpe generating plant is due to be commissioned during 2010.

North of Newark and on the tidal part of the Trent are, or were, three more stations. The first, at High Marnham, fed the National Grid for almost 45 years between 1959 and closure in 2003. The final two, at Cottam and West Burton, which are less than five miles from each other, are both still generating. Each can potentially supply over 2,000 megawatts to the grid.

This chain of ten power stations in their heyday provided an awesome amount of electricity to Britain's homes. Equally, to supply this demand, they consumed a prodigious amount of coal … coal that was delivered by rail. So a vital factor in the selection of all the Trent Valley power station sites was the proximity of a railway line. Of the 'big five' in Nottinghamshire, Ratcliffe was adjacent to the original Midland

Counties Railway of 1840. Staythorpe was supplied from George Stephenson's Nottingham to Lincoln line. High Marnham relied on fuel carried on the former Lancashire, Derbyshire & East Coast Railway. The old Great Central Retford to Lincoln line supplies fuel to Cottam, whilst the GCR Retford to Gainsborough line caters for West Burton's needs.

Against this background of the power stations' appetite for coal, it is easy to see why the nationalised NCB and BR were prepared to make such heavy investments in the post-war Nottinghamshire pits and their associated branch lines.

THE COLLIERY LINES

Not unnaturally, with the abundance of 'free' fuel, many collieries continued to use steam locomotives long after their larger main line siblings had been despatched into

New Hucknall Colliery on 4th April 1969. It was Good Friday and two of the colliery's steam locomotives are enjoying a day off in the spring sunshine. Both had previously been employed at other collieries. NCB no 36 (on the right) was one of 377 similar 'Austerity' locomotives produced during the Second World War. Although designed by the Hunslet Engine Co, many were built by other private contractors, including no 36 (works number 5286), which was built by the Vulcan Foundry as Ministry of Supply no 72596 at Newton-le-Willows as the war was drawing to a close. After the cessation of hostilities, the LNER bought 75 of these for use as shunting locomotives, which they classified as 'J94'. Many of the remainder were eventually sold for further service in collieries, docks, steelworks etc. A further 107 of these simple, robust and easily maintained locos continued to be built until 1964. Prior to moving to New Hucknall, no 36 had worked at Moor Green Colliery. Behind it is Swanwick Colliery No 5, which had served just across the border in Derbyshire for many years after being built in Bristol by Peckett & Co as no 1972 in 1940. (Photograph courtesy of Richard Stevens)

oblivion, or the few fortunate ones had gone into preservation. A lot depended on the management's attitude to steam and the willingness of staff to continue using steam.

For the old-timers there was a kind of understandable love-hate relationship. If you loved steam, you put up with the downsides. Probably typical of this breed of engineman was the late Lionel Gadsby, a larger than life character who was a driver at Castle Donington Power Station and who I was privileged to meet. Thanks to Lionel and his colleagues, steam reigned supreme at the power station until the 1990s.

Lionel had a very philosophical outlook about the two steam locos that he drove. For a start, they were dirty: 'You were up to your neck in filth and coal dust. When the wind blew it was draughty. When it rained you got wet. When it was hot you sweated.' But, for Lionel, driving the standby diesels was as impersonal as driving a car. On the other hand he looked on the two steamers that he drove as living machines. 'You could do anything with them, and they would do anything for you. The power was always there when you needed it; they never let you down.'

After the withdrawal of the last steam locomotives from BR in August 1968, the continued use of steam by the NCB and others tended to be ignored by many enthusiasts. My friend Richard Stevens was one of those who bucked the trend and often explored the private NCB lines. It was not without problems. Richard recalls that the day he took the photograph on page 105 in 1969 he had earlier been detained by a security officer at another colliery as a suspected IRA terrorist … even though he was still in his teens and his mode of transport was a push bike!

Since the 1970s, coal mining has been in a terminal decline throughout the UK and has now all but vanished from Nottinghamshire. Indeed, Welbeck Colliery closed in May 2010 as I was writing this very chapter. This leaves just one pit, Thoresby, still in operation. It has reserves that it is anticipated will last until 2017. Harworth Colliery in the north of the county, which was mothballed in 2006, also has significant reserves. Its long-term future, however, is still under consideration by its owners, UK Coal.

A graphic illustration of the downside of steam. At the end of a shift with a diesel you simply applied the handbrake, hit the 'Stop Engine' button and opened the battery switch. After that you could clock off and head for a pint in the 'miners' welfare' or a local pub. At the end of a steam shift there was still work to be done. There was the red-hot clinker to remove from the ash pan underneath the loco. There was the hot dusty char to be emptied from the smokebox, as is being carried out in this photograph at Bestwood Colliery. The loco, no 3, which was named Felix, *had been built by Andrew Barclay & Co in Kilmarnock in 1954 (works no 2344). Before the steam crew could finally clock off, the boiler had to be filled, the fire backed up for the night and left with all the dampers closed so the loco could be 'brought round' (easily get steam up again) the following day. I guess the first pint wouldn't have touched the sides when the steam crew eventually got into the 'welfare'.* (Photograph courtesy of Richard Stevens)

11

DECLINE

Most historians agree that the British railway system reached its zenith in the years immediately preceding the First World War. Even so, competition from electric tramways was beginning to be felt. As early as 1911 the station at Lenton on the Leen Valley line was closed as a result of the tramway extension into this suburb of Nottingham.

For the duration of both the 1914–1918 and 1939–1945 conflicts the railways came under Government control, albeit that the Railway Executive Committee, charged with the running of the system, was made up of highly respected senior railway managers, rather than politicians. But both the wars put an intolerable strain on the railways from which, on both occasions, they never fully recovered.

In the aftermath of the First World War, the hundred or so previously independent railways found themselves merged into one of the 'Big Four' in 1923. In turn, the 'Big Four' faced a similar situation after the Second World War. This ultimately led to the nationalisation of the railways on 1st January 1948.

An early casualty of World War I was the Nottingham Suburban Railway; the little used stations at Thorneywood, St Ann's Well and Sherwood closed their doors as a wartime economy measure on 13th July 1916. The closure was to be permanent. Two weeks previously, Linby station on the GNR's Leen Valley line had also closed. This too was to be permanent.

The Midland Railway's lines in Nottinghamshire were not immune either. The 'Penny Emma' service on the ¾ mile branch between Sutton Junction and Sutton-in-Ashfield was withdrawn on 1st January 1917. This proved to be only temporary, the service eventually being reinstated in 1923.

Not so lucky were the passenger services over the MR Basford and Bennerley line, which were also withdrawn on New Year's Day 1917. This time the surgery was somewhat more drastic as over a mile of both the up and down lines west of Kimberley were lifted and shipped to France for reuse at the Front. That said, local legend has it that the boat carrying the rails was torpedoed and sunk in the Channel.

These wartime closures were to prove to be the 'tip of the iceberg', yet their

The Great Northern's Linby station photographed in happier times with a departing northbound local train seen in the distance getting to grips with the 1 in 70 gradient to the next station at Newstead. At the end of the platform is Linby North signalbox with its decorative bargeboards, behind which is a typical GNR somersault signal. The elevated 'hut' on the left hand side of the signalbox contains the signalman's toilet, known in the trade as a 'thunder box'. The lattice girder bridge beyond the end of the platform carries the Great Central main line.
(Courtesy of R.H. Bird and Picture the Past)

impact was minimal. The more convenient Nottingham Corporation trams had made inroads into the Nottingham Suburban's passenger traffic whilst the inhabitants of Linby, Sutton and Kimberley were all served by other railway companies: the Midland at Linby, the GNR at Kimberley and both the GNR and GCR at Sutton.

Kimberley was also served by trams, this time the privately owned Nottinghamshire & Derbyshire Tramway Co, which was an early subsidiary of today's multi-national Balfour Beatty. This line ran for 15 miles from the centre of Nottingham to Ripley, over the border in Derbyshire. The trams, known as the 'Ripley Rattlers' were immortalised by D.H. Lawrence in the short story *Tickets Please*, which he wrote in 1919. Derailments and accidents were commonplace and the system gained the reputation of the country's most dangerous tramway. Another local legend has it that the first tram got jammed under the GNR railway bridge spanning Main Street in Kimberley. As a consequence the road and tramlines had to be lowered. There must be some truth in the story as a dip in the road is still visible today.

The impact of the First World War on the railways was profound. It was a triple

The Midland Railway's Kimberley station in the days when Nottingham to Ilkeston passenger trains stopped here and before the line towards Bennerley was lifted and shipped to France. Dominating the skyline is Hanson's Brewery. Out of sight, to the left of the photographer, is the equally large Hardy's Brewery. Both were served by separate sidings from the Midland line. Freight services to Kimberley were withdrawn as early as 1951, after which the station building became Kimberley Ex-Servicemen's Club. That too has now closed, but the station building, although rather derelict, was still standing in May 2010. (Courtesy of A.P. Knighton and Picture the Past)

whammy. First was the tragic loss of the thousands of railwaymen who were killed in action. Secondly, whilst the railways had responded magnificently and were a vital component in the allied victory, after the Armistice, the lack of maintenance and investment during the conflict really began to take its toll. To enable the 100 or so independent railway companies to 'recover' they were amalgamated into one of the 'Big Four' railways on 1st January 1923. The Midland and the London & North Western found themselves in the LMS group, whilst the Great Central and the Great Northern became part of the LNER. The Nottingham Suburban Railway, and the Nottingham & Grantham Railway & Canal Co, both of which were worked by the GNR, naturally followed their leader into the LNER.

But perhaps the most insidious element was that during the four years of conflict, great strides had been made in the reliability of the internal combustion engine and the consequent construction of thousands of motor vehicles. Slowly, but surely, these began to be cascaded from military into civilian use. Demobbed lorries began to take goods directly from A to B – doorstep to doorstep, or factory to factory, without any intermediate help from the railways. In many cases this road transport was both quicker and cheaper. Other ex-War Department vehicles could be quite easily converted into buses or charabancs.

For the railways it was the thin edge of the wedge and we do not need to look very far to find a classic example …

For going on 70 years, buses owned by W. Gash & Sons were a familiar sight in and around Newark and on the roads from there into Nottingham. The story began in 1918, when William Gash, who was the proprietor of the corn mill in the village of Elston, bought a second-hand lorry to carry his wares to and from Newark Market. Soon after acquiring the lorry, Elston's joiner-cum-undertaker hired Mr Gash's lorry to take an empty coffin to Newark Hospital and return with the body of a deceased villager. According to his daughter, it seems that during the journey Mr Gash got the idea that he could not only carry dead villagers in his lorry, there was scope for carrying live ones too. To cut the story short, the joiner produced some slatted benches, which were fitted into the back of the lorry. The local blacksmith became involved too by forging a number of semi-circular hoops for the lorry, over which a tarpaulin could be draped to give the passengers some measure of protection in inclement weather. Thus the W. Gash & Sons bus service was born.

As noted above, the 'Penny Emma' passenger service between Sutton Junction and Sutton-in-Ashfield was reinstated by the LMS in 1923 after a gap of six years. Three years later the 'plug was pulled again' as a result of the General Strike in 1926. Other branch line services elsewhere on the LMS system were similarly 'temporarily' withdrawn due to the strike. In the event, many of these 'temporary' closures became permanent, but the Sutton Town branch bucked this trend by reopening again after a break of just over four months. From then on the 'Penny Emma' remained a familiar part of Sutton life until advertised services were finally withdrawn in 1949. Unadvertised workmen's trains, however, continued for a further two years.

The next victim on the LMS closure list was the passenger service between Southwell and Mansfield. It has to be said that few tears were shed at the loss in August 1929. The service was dreadfully slow. Local legend has it that on some services it was possible to get off the train at Rainworth, have a couple of beers in the nearby pub before resuming the journey on the same train. The intermediate stations did remain open until 1965 for occasional race specials to Rolleston Junction, which is alongside the Southwell Racecourse.

The LNER was next to wield the axe. For many Nottinghamshire folk, 14th September 1931 was a black day. This was the date that the doors at Scrooby station on the ECML were closed and locked for the final time, as were the doors of Checker House station on the former GCR Sheffield to Retford line. Even more significant was the complete withdrawal of the local passenger services on the GNR's Leen Valley line from Nottingham to Annesley and then beyond, on the extension line from Kirkby South Junction to Langwith.

The LNER did attempt to reduce its operating costs on some rural branch lines by introducing steam-powered railcars, built by the Sentinel Waggon Works at Shrewsbury. Over the years several were allocated to Colwick for use on Nottinghamshire's local services. But in reality, it was too little, too late. Certainly the Sentinel railcars were cheaper to operate, but the savings they offered were minimal in comparison with the overall costs of operating and maintaining a line. Nobody seemed to want to grasp the nettle of closing stations and making them into unstaffed halts. Indeed even after the withdrawal of regular passenger services, many stations remained open for freight and the occasional special excursions. The withdrawal of passenger services may have resulted in one or two members of staff being made redundant, or redeployed, but the annual accounts still included many unnecessary staff wages.

Second World War

As in World War I, the railways were immediately taken into Government control, through a Railway Executive Committee that once again was made up of men drawn from the top echelons of railway management. One of their first acts was to withdraw the passenger service between Newark and Nottingham Victoria. In reality, the only casualty was Cotham as the stations on the Grantham line remained open. And it probably came as no surprise to the residents of Cotham because during the war the REC had closed the station for two years.

Another early REC edict was the withdrawal of catering vehicles and the unnaming of the 'prestige' trains like the *Coronation* and *The Queen of Scots* on the ECML and *The Thames-Clyde* and *The Thames-Forth* expresses on the Midland main line.

In many ways the result of the Second World War was a re-run of the 1914–1918 conflict. Once again, many railwaymen were sadly killed in action. Again too, the railways played a vital part in the allied victory, but as after the First World War, by 1945 the lack of maintenance and investment was taking a heavy toll. Just as the aftermath of the First World War had forced the railways to amalgamate into the 'Big Four', the four became one with the nationalisation of the railways on 1st January 1948.

But once again, the technological advances that had been made in response to the demands of the war were to have serious repercussions for the railways once the victory celebrations were over. This time it was the mass production techniques that had been evolved to satisfy the war effort that were the problem. The production of motor vehicles for civilian use during the war had all but ceased, but by 1946 updated versions of the pre-war Ford Prefect and Ford Anglia were beginning to roll off the assembly lines at Dagenham. In 1948, Morris Motors unveiled the first Morris Minor; this was designed by Alec Issigonis, who went on to achieve greater fame (and a knighthood) for his Mini, which was launched in 1959. By 1960, one in nine households owned a car. With a 'basic' Mini costing under £500, the 1 to 9 ratio was decreasing rapidly. But it has to be said, however, that a 'basic' Mini lacked 'accessories' that today we take for granted such a heater and wing mirrors!

The bottom line invariably meant that every car sold, either new or second-hand, represented a potential loss of revenue to the railways. Families who had previously travelled to Teignmouth or Bournemouth or to Yarmouth or Weymouth and to dozens of other resorts, north, south, east and west, by train for their annual holidays now packed the luggage and the kids into their Ford 'Pop' or their Austin A40 or their Hillman Minx and went by road instead. Who could blame them? Perhaps it wasn't always quicker by road, but it was certainly more convenient, and usually cheaper. When I began driving in the mid 1960s a gallon of petrol cost around 5 shillings, which equates today to under 6p a litre.

The late 1940s and early 1950s saw piecemeal closures. Upper Broughton on the Midland line to Melton closed in 1948, whilst its neighbours at Widmerpool and Plumtree both closed a year later. On the East Coast Main Line, Barnby Moor & Sutton (where Alan Pegler watched the inaugural run of the non-stop *Flying Scotsman*) locked its doors to passengers in November 1949. Passenger trains also stopped calling at the little used interchange station with the Lancashire, Derbyshire & East Coast line, Dukeries Junction, in March 1950. Other ECML closures were Carlton-on-Trent (1953), Tuxford (1955), whilst Crow Park and Ranskill both succumbed in 1958, leaving just Newark and Retford open for business.

Space precludes a complete list of pre-Beeching closures, but the more significant ones include the former GNR/LNWR Joint line in December 1953 and the old LD&ECR line from Langwith Juction (by then renamed Shirebrook North) to Lincoln. One final noteworthy pre-Beeching closure was the sudden withdrawal of all services, passenger and freight, through the 1,132 yard long Mapperley Tunnel on the GNR 'Back Line' on 4th April 1960, due to safety fears about the tunnel's structural stability due to mining subsidence.

It was not the first time. Back in January 1925, over 30 feet of the tunnel roof had collapsed, burying the line in bricks and earth. Until repairs were completed, the Nottingham Suburban Railway was used as a diversion, but by 1960, as related in Chapter 3, the NSR was no longer an option. This time the tunnel never reopened.

Doctor Beeching

The blame for the wholesale closures of many of Britain's railways is often attributed to Richard Beeching, Chairman of the British Railways Board from 1961 to 1965. Yet, as noted earlier in the chapter, the LMS, LNER and early British Railways managements had started the job by at least pruning services on some unremunerative branch lines and closing uneconomic stations.

Beeching, a very able engineer and a clever physicist, was Technical Director of ICI when he was seconded for five years by the Government to try to sort out the financial mess that BR were in. His brief was not only to reduce the increasing year-on-year losses being sustained by the railways, but to bring them back into profit. It was a tough call for someone without any previous professional railway experience.

In 1955, the British Railways Board's predecessor, the British Transport Commission, had produced a so called 'Modernisation Plan'. In essence, the plan was based on the naive premise that increased speeds, improved reliability and better safety would result in passengers and freight customers returning in droves to using the railways, and consequently taking them back into profitability. One of the key elements was the replacement of steam by diesel or electric traction.

The plan was fatally flawed. BR began ordering hundreds of untried and untested designs of diesel and electric locomotives, many from private contractors. Some of the designs ultimately proved to be a good investment. Others were nothing less than a total disaster in terms of reliability and soon disappeared from the railway scene, albeit at a tremendous cost to the taxpayer. That was only a fraction of the story of waste and unwise investment. So instead of being in profit by 1962, as predicted by the Modernisation Plan, BR's balance sheet showed a loss of £104 million ... an increase of £17 million over the previous year's deficit. On the face of it, Beeching's task was 'mission impossible'.

The 1955 Modernisation Plan had failed to grasp the fundamental fact that many of Britain's railways had passed their 'best before' date, and assumed that investing

Nottingham Midland station in pre-Beeching days. The train standing at Platform 5 on Sunday 6th May 1956 is the RCTS's East Midlander *preparing to depart for a visit to the former Great Western Works at Swindon. The loco, a former Midland Railway 2P 4-4-0, no 40454, was based at Nottingham and has been specially cleaned and polished for the occasion. The little loco has a long day ahead of it. The outward journey was via Birmingham and Cheltenham, returning via Oxford, Bletchley and Wellinborough, the 2P working the train throughout. No wonder the tender is piled high with coal! For the steeply graded section over the former Midland & South Western Junction line between Cheltenham and Swindon, sister loco no 40489 acted as the pilot loco. The sight and sound of the two veterans blasting their way through the Cotswolds must have been unforgettable.*
(J.F. Henton, courtesy of the C.A. Turner Collection)

£millions on upgrades would reverse the defection of passengers and freight onto the roads. Beeching was handed a 'poisoned chalice'. He responded by publishing in March 1963 his infamous report *The Reshaping of British Railways*. It was highly controversial. It proposed closing all unprofitable lines; over 2,000 stations would close and 70,000 employees would be removed from the payroll.

For many Notts folk, the most controversial of Beeching's proposals was the closure of the GCR London Extension and Nottingham Victoria.

When the railways were nationalised in 1948, the former LNER lines became part of the Eastern Region, whilst the old LMS lines found themselves in the London

Midland Region. At the time it was a logical division, but in 1958 BR decided to redraw the boundaries on a geographical, rather than on a historical basis. Thus, except for a small pocket around Sheffield, the GCR London Extension came under the London Midland's jurisdiction. When, 35 years after the grouping and 10 years on from nationalisation, the long despised GCR fell into their laps, the London Midland diehards could not believe their luck. For the London Extension it was the kiss of death. It is a long and painful story, starting with the LMR withdrawing through expresses from Manchester to London Marylebone at the beginning of January 1960. Thus when the line came under scrutiny by Dr Beeching and his financial analysts it became a prime target for closure.

The slow and painful death spanned several years. When Victoria closed, Arkwright Street was reopened again to serve as the terminus for the pathetic substitute diesel railcar service to Rugby. It seemed that the London Midland management were trying to inflict the maximum humiliation on its former rival until it was finally despatched to oblivion.

The closure is still mourned by many. But the section from Ruddington through south Nottinghamshire to the outskirts of Loughborough has been preserved, as has the separate section from Loughborough into the northern suburbs of Leicester, to remind future generations of a once great main line.

Other proposals in Beeching's report made equally unpalatable reading for Notts folk.

The former GNR lines to Ilkeston and Derby along with the Pinxton branch were on Beeching's hit list. The former Midland lines were not immune either. Local passenger services to Derby, Leicester, Sheffield (via the Erewash Valley), Worksop (via the Leen Valley) and to Lincoln were all proposed to be withdrawn along the intermediate stations *en route*.

Ranking equally with the GCR closures was the proposed complete closure of the Midland line to Melton Mowbray.

In the event, the local services on the Midland lines to Lincoln and Derby survived Beeching's axe. But in effect, the clock was being turned back 100 years because in respect of fast inter-city trains, Nottingham was again at the end of a branch line.

But at least Nottingham was still served by passenger trains. Mansfield was denied that luxury, resulting in it becoming the largest town in the country without a passenger service. As if to rub salt into the wounds, BR reopened a station **nine** miles away in the Erewash Valley, which they named Alfreton & Mansfield Parkway.

In retrospect, in many ways Beeching did the country a favour. How could it be justified for three separate railways to run cheek by jowl, crossing and re-crossing each other as in the confines of the Leen Valley? The answer is that it couldn't.

But as we will see in the final chapter, Beeching was not infallible ...

Fast Forward

The Notts railway network today

Give or take a few exceptions, the railway map of Nottinghamshire today is almost identical to those that were drawn in the 1850s and 1860s. As is so often the case elsewhere, many of Nottinghamshire's later railways have been victims of the 'last-in–first-out' principle.

Most of the Midland Railway's early routes are still intact, as are the Great Northern's East Coast Main Line (1852) and the 1849 branch line from Nottingham to Grantham. Similarly, the Manchester, Sheffield & Lincolnshire line that put both Worksop and Retford on the railway maps in 1849 is still going strong.

Of particular interest today is the former MR line between Nottingham and Worksop. As noted in the previous chapter, passenger services along the 32 mile route were among the many victims of Dr Beeching's infamous axe, closure coming in October 1964. Mineral traffic from the Leen Valley collieries continued, but as one by one these pits closed, the future began to look very bleak indeed.

Kirkby Tunnel under Robin Hood Hills at Annesley was closed in 1970; the rails were lifted and the tunnel and its approach cuttings were filled with colliery waste.

But then a miracle happened. OK, perhaps 'miracle' might be a bit of an exaggeration, but it began to dawn on the civic authorities along the route that Beeching had got it badly wrong. The full story is way beyond my steam railways in Nottinghamshire remit, but passenger services on the former MR Leen Valley line between Nottingham and Newstead were reinstated in May 1993.

Three and a half years later, the colliery and landfill rubbish blocking Kirkby Tunnel had not only been removed, the tunnel itself was found to be in excellent condition. As a result, passenger services were extended to Mansfield Woodhouse. The final section to Worksop opened in May 1998. It was perhaps inevitable, given the deep involvement of Nottinghamshire County Council in financing the project, that the reopened route would be called the 'Robin Hood Line'.

The level crossing at the south end of the Midland's station at Kirkby, which can be seen in the photograph on page 118, had long been a constant source of annoyance to the locals, as had one to the north of station. With dwindling traffic in the early

The former Midland Railway station at Kirkby-in-Ashfield is seen here on a sunny day in the 1950s with 2P 4-4-0 no 40454 piloting an unidentified 4F 0-6-0 on a local Mansfield to Nottingham passenger service. It is highly unlikely that the train would have actually required two locomotives. A more probable reason is that one of the two locos in the picture was needed at Nottingham and to save finding a path for a light engine movement, this 'double-header' had been organised. (Frank Ashley)

1970s, British Railways decided to rationalise the former Midland, Great Northern and Great Central routes through the town to eliminate Kirkby's level crossings.

The bottom line to this rationalisation is that today after leaving Kirkby Tunnel the Robin Hood Line diverts first to follow the course of the Great Central … albeit the lines of which originally were some 30 feet below. At a point close to the site of the original Kirkby South Junction, the Robin Hood Line switches its route along the former Great Northern Leen Valley Extension. Here in the former GNR cutting a brand new Kirkby station has been built (the GNR never bothered to build a station at Kirkby). Finally, after the new station, Robin Hood trains use the link back to the original MR line constructed by BR in 1972 to enable the closure of the Kirkby level crossings to take place.

Some reminders of the past

Due to space limitations it is impossible to present a comprehensive review of every surviving relic from the age of steam in Nottinghamshire, but I have included some of the more notable and interesting ones below.

The most spectacular omission from today's railway maps has to be the Great Central's London Extension, which strode boldly and indiscriminately through the county, and indeed through Nottingham itself. Any obstacle in its course was summarily dealt with. But, as the saying goes, 'every dog has its day' and the resulting retribution has resulted in most evidence of the line, particularly in Nottingham and to the north of the city, being despatched into total oblivion.

The one exception north of the city is the almost buried north portal of Sherwood Rise Tunnel (OS ref SK564422). It is to be found hidden amongst some trees at the end of a small narrow grassed recreation area beyond Camelot Drive. I had travelled through the tunnel by train on several occasions before the line closed, but visiting the site over 40 years later was for me an eerie and rather uncomfortable experience. I cannot explain the discomfort, unless it was because the tunnel itself is reputed to be haunted.

A young couple that I spoke to, who lived nearby and whose small sons were happily kicking a football about on the grass, had absolutely no idea that there were the remains of a railway tunnel, hidden in the trees, just yards away from where they were sitting. Similarly they hadn't realised that the steep rock faces that flanked their children's play area had originally formed a railway cutting. But thinking about it since, I suspect that many Notts folk born after the mid 1960s will not have much, if indeed any, inkling that a once great railway ran through their midst.

For instance, I wonder how many of the shoppers visiting the large Morrison supermarket at Bulwell (SK544460) realise that once upon a time trains roared high above the site on the mighty GCR Bulwell Viaduct. Equally, I am sure that few of the students attending New College Nottingham's Clarendon Campus (SK568416) will be aware that it is built on the infilled cutting between Sherwood Rise and Mansfield Road Tunnels where once was located the Great Central's Carrington station.

In a similar vein, I guess that many of the young shoppers eagerly spending their money in Nottingham's Victoria Centre shops have little or no idea that the complex occupies a good deal of the former Victoria station site. Yet from the shopping centre car parks, the southern portal of Mansfield Road Tunnel is still easily visible as a reminder of the GCR, as are some of the walls and sheer sides of the sandstone cutting that once surrounded the station. More poignant perhaps is the 100 foot high clock tower that once dominated the station entrance. Happily, the developers decided to retain the tower and the clock and incorporate it into the new shopping centre. That said, it now sits rather incongruously in its 'new' surroundings and is dwarfed by the hideous tower block of flats that the city planners allowed to be built on the site. Indeed, the redevelopment has been described as 'one of the worst blights ever inflicted on any British city'. I stress that these are NOT my words, but ones that I do not disagree with. But the clock tower is a tangible reminder, at least for the older residents of the city, of the once great station that occupied the site.

Victoria Street Tunnel to the south of the station, which caused the contractor so much trouble, still exists. But the only evidence of it today is a small, insignificant access door to the north end, hidden in the bowels of the Victoria Centre car park. For many years after closure, the south end of the tunnel was visible at Weekday Cross, but since 2007 this too has now disappeared, hidden by the new CCAN (Centre for Contemporary Arts Nottingham) building. Yet the tunnel is still in use ... and for steam! It provides a route for the steam pipes from the municipal waste incinerator at nearby Eastcroft, which heat the Victoria Centre and premises nearby.

Continuing a short distance south from Weekday Cross, there is another small reminder of the London Extension. These are the last remaining arches of the once massive blue brick and girder viaducts that carried the GCR high above the city, over the Midland's station and onwards across the Trent towards London. These six remaining arches have been 'recycled' and now form the present southern terminus of the Nottingham Express Tramway (NET) system.

Ironically it is now proposed to construct replacement viaducts over Station Street, the Midland station, and beyond, on the line of the long demolished Great Central ones to accommodate the tracks for the southern and western extensions to the NET. Not surprisingly, the reconstruction of these will cost megabucks. To offset part of these costs it is proposed that these lines will be partly financed by a highly controversial business car parking levy. The groundswell of public opinion against such a levy is gaining momentum. We will just have to wait and see ...

Before leaving Nottingham I must mention the Great Northern's long disused Low Level station on London Road (SK580393), which in spite of years of neglect and vandalism has survived virtually intact and is now enjoying a new lease of life as a fitness centre. All traces of its successor, London Road High Level (Alight here for Trent Bridge Cricket and Football Grounds!) have vanished except for less than 50 yards of the viaduct between Popham Street and Maltmill Lane (SK575396) that once carried the line to Weekday Cross and on into Victoria.

Vying with London Road Low Level station as the most significant remaining GNR artefact in Nottinghamshire, is Bennerley Viaduct. Over this, the GNR strode across the Erewash Valley to challenge the Midland Railway on its home ground (SK475440). Bombs dropped from a German Zeppelin during the First World War failed to even damage it. Subsequent plans to demolish the structure, after the line across it was closed in 1968, have been equally unsuccessful.

As related in Chapter 5, because of the unpredictable and unstable nature of the ground beneath the viaduct, a relatively lightweight wrought iron lattice structure was utilised. Not only did the resulting open structure allow the blast waves from the Zeppelin's bombs to pass through harmlessly, the scrap metal men invited to tender for the demolition of the viaduct probably took one look, and after a sharp intake of breath, either said 'no way' or quoted an astronomical price for the work.

The reason was, and still is, that wrought iron structures have to be dismantled rivet by rivet. Oxy-acetylene torches have little or no effect. So rather than spend megabucks on its removal, the relevant authorities, perhaps reluctantly, have allowed it to remain. In doing so, the historical importance of Bennerley Viaduct has subsequently been recognised and although it is currently categorised as being 'at risk' it has a Grade II* listing. It is one of only two remaining wrought iron viaducts in the UK. The other is the Meldon Viaduct in Devon.

Two very other significant Nottinghamshire railway viaducts have survived into the 21st century. One is at Fledborough (SK816715), which consists of 59 blue brick arches across the Trent floodplain and is some 800 yards long. The second is King's Mill Viaduct in Mansfield (SK519598). Constructed by the Mansfield & Pinxton Railway in 1818, it now lays claim to be the oldest surviving railway viaduct in the country. This fact is acknowledged by it having a Grade II listing.

More a bridge than a viaduct, are the three spans at Lady Bay (SK584387) over which the Midland's line to Melton Mowbray crossed the Trent after leaving Nottingham station. Following the closure of the Melton line, the bridge became part of the A6011 road, which along with a new separate footpath for pedestrians opened in December 1979.

Stations

Memories of the golden age of Nottinghamshire's railways can be rekindled by visiting some of the surviving structures that have fortunately survived into the 21st century.

The 'jewel in the crown' architecturally has to be the Midland Railway's 1904 station in the city itself (SK575393), which has a Grade II* listing. Part of the Neo-Baroque façade with its central clock tower on Carrington Street can be seen in the photograph overleaf.

On the opposite side of Carrington Street, on the city side of the former MR Goods Offices (now the Coroner's Office) are the stone gateposts of the original 1839 Midland Counties station.

Although all have now been altered to varying degrees, I find it quite easy to forget the modern images present at Worksop (SK585797), Mansfield (SK537608) and both Newark's stations, and travel back in time to the great days of steam. For me, the

Nottingham Midland station seen here on 13th September 1987, nearly 20 years after BR withdrew its last steam locomotives. The preserved BR Standard class 4MT 4-6-0, no 75069, is pulling out of Platform 1 with the 'Derwent Valley Explorer', one of several similar excursion trains organised by BR around that time. (Photograph courtesy of Richard Stevens)

most poignant reminder has to be the wonderful Potts of Leeds clock on the down platform at Newark Northgate (Chapter 8).

The Midland Railway's 1846 line from Nottingham to Lincoln has many original buildings, although most are now privately owned. My favourites are the buildings at Thurgarton (SK698485) and Lowdham (SK674459).

PRESERVATION

There are two preserved railways in Nottinghamshire. One is a heritage line. The other is somewhat higher tech!

The heritage line, the Great Central Railway (Nottingham), is based at Ruddington and runs steam and diesel hauled services (mainly at weekends), along a 10 mile stretch of the former GCR London Extension between Ruddington and the outskirts of Loughborough. Operated by volunteers, the ultimate aim is to link up with the 'other' Great Central Railway, which runs south from Loughborough to Leicester. The gap between the two lines is tantalisingly short, but the key element … and the one that will cost £millions … is a new bridge spanning the Midland main line.

As with many heritage railways, diesel as well as steam locos are used to haul the trains on the GCR(N). To avoid disappointment, prospective visitors are recommended to check with the railway before starting out; the telephone number is 0115 940 5705.

The Old Dalby Test Track

I have no doubt that many steam enthusiasts will throw their hands up in horror at my inclusion of the Old Dalby in this review. But the bottom line is that it **is** a **preserved railway** and it is part of the Nottinghamshire railway scene today – albeit one that is dedicated to the future, rather than to the past.

Following final closure of the former Midland Railway Nottingham and Melton line in 1967, the part of the line between Edwalton and Melton Mowbray was handed over to the Advanced Projects section of BR's Research Department. It has subsequently become known as the Old Dalby Test Track.

Initially, it was used for testing the prototype of the Advanced Passenger Train (APT-E). Powered by gas turbines, it set out to prove the concept that significantly higher speeds could be safely and comfortably achieved on existing tracks by means of tilting the carriages as they negotiated curves. Between 1973 and 1976 the APT-E became a familiar sight streaking through the pastoral scenery of rural Nottinghamshire and on into Leicestershire. On one occasion in 1976, it reached 143.6 mph.

Some years after the retirement of the APT-E to the National Railway Museum, perhaps the most spectacular and much publicised 'research' test took place in July 1984. In front of invited guests and watched by the world's press and television cameras, BR staged a crash between an empty and driverless passenger train travelling at between 90 and 100 mph and a nuclear waste flask. The crash was carried out to prove the integrity of such flasks in the event of a serious collision. The locomotive and coaches were damaged beyond repair by the impact. The flask remained intact.

Following privatisation of the railways and the fragmentation of the former BR Research Dept, the line was leased by Alstom for testing the new tilting Pendolino trains ordered by Richard Branson's Virgin Trains prior to them entering service on the West Coast Main Line. But in order to do this, a large part of the test track had to be electrified in 2001 with 25kV overhead lines.

The irony of the situation was that due to political indifference and the consequential lack of funding, BR's own tilting Advanced Passenger Train project was scrapped. Now, some 25 years later, that same line on which the early tests were carried out was being used to test what many consider is an inferior Italian designed tilting train, albeit one that utilised many features copied from the BR original.

Following another period of uncertainty after Alstom pulled out of the UK, Old Dalby was taken over by Metronet, the troubled joint private and public finance company charged with the modernisation of London Underground. So now, in addition to being equipped with 25kV ac overhead lines, a section has been electrified with third and fourth rails at 750 volts dc for testing the next generation of underground trains.

Just as the APT-E was a once a familiar sight on the Old Dalby line, an unwary traveller today might blink twice at seeing a 'lost' London Underground train travelling so far from home through the pastoral Nottinghamshire landscape.

The rise and fall of the Great Central Railway's London Extension has formed quite a significant part of this book. So for me, this superb image of a train, reflected in the still waters of the River Soar, as it steams across the former GCR Stanford Viaduct, out of Nottinghamshire and into Leicestershire, is an excellent way of saying 'au revoir'. (Photograph courtesy of Richard Stevens)

Bibliography

Anderson, P. Howard *Forgotten Railways – The East Midlands* David & Charles, Newton Abbot 1973

Anderson, Paul & Cupit J. *An Illustrated History of Mansfield's Railways* Irwell Press 2000

Bell, David *Memories of the Nottinghamshire Coalfields* Countryside Books, Newbury 2008

Cupit, J. & Taylor, W. *The Lancashire, Derbyshire & East Coast Railway* Oakwood Press 1966

Daniels, G. & Dench, L. *Passengers No More* Ian Allan, London 1980

Elliott, B.J. *South Yorkshire Joint Railway & the Coalfield* Oakwood Press 2002

Forster, V. & Taylor, W. *Railways in and around Nottingham* Foxline, Stockport 1991

Haresnape, Brian *Fowler Locomotives* Ian Allan, London 1972

Haresnape, Brian *Ivatt & Riddles Locomotives* Ian Allan, London 1977

Hawkins, C. & Reeve, G. *LMS Engine Sheds Vol 2: The Midland Railway* Wild Swan Publications 1981

Henshaw, Alfred *The Great Northern Railway in the East Midlands 1* RCTS 1999

Henshaw, Alfred *The Great Northern Railway in the East Midlands 2* RCTS 2000

Henshaw, Alfred *The Great Northern Railway in the East Midlands 3* RCTS 2000

Henshaw, Alfred *The Great Northern Railway in the East Midlands 4* RCTS 2003

Hurst, Geoffrey *The Midland Railway around Nottinghamshire* Milepost Publications, Worksop

Kingscott, Geoffrey *Lost Railways of Nottinghamshire* Countryside Books, Newbury 2005

Leleux, Robin *Regional History of the Railways of GB Vol 9* David & Charles, Newton Abbot 1976

Lund, Brian *Nottinghamshire Railway Stations* Reflections of a Bygone Age, Keyworth 1991

Midland Railway *Distance Diagrams (Reprint) Vol 2* Peter Kay, Teignmouth

Nock, O.S. *LNER Steam* Pan Books/David & Charles 1971

Vanags, John *The Mansfield & Pinxton Railway* Old Mansfield Society 2000

Vanns, Michael A. *Rail Centres – Nottingham* Book Law Publications, Nottingham 2004

Vanns, Michael A. *Railways of Newark-on-Trent* Oakwood Press, Usk 1999

Waite, Peter B. *Railways of Nottingham* Book Law Publications 2004

Walker, Colin *Great Central Twilight* Pendyke Publications, Llangollen 1986

Yeadon, W.B. *Register of LNER Locomotives Vol 1A1 & A3* Irwell Press 1990

Index

Index